DevOps for Salesforce

Build, test, and streamline data pipelines to simplify
development in Salesforce

Priyanka Dive
Nagraj Gornalli

BIRMINGHAM - MUMBAI

DevOps for Salesforce

Commissioning Editor: Aaron Lazar
Acquisition Editor: Karan Sadawana, Denim Pinto
Content Development Editor: Rohit Kumar Singh
Technical Editor: Ketan Kamble
Copy Editor: Safis Editing
Project Coordinator: Vaidehi Sawant
Proofreader: Safis Editing
Indexer: Rekha Nair
Graphics: Alishon Mendonsa
Production Coordinator: Arvindkumar Gupta

First published: September 2018

Production reference: 1290918

Published by Packt Publishing Ltd.
Livery Place
35 Livery Street
Birmingham
B3 2PB, UK.

ISBN 978-1-78883-334-9

www.packtpub.com

`mapt.io`

Mapt is an online digital library that gives you full access to over 5,000 books and videos, as well as industry leading tools to help you plan your personal development and advance your career. For more information, please visit our website.

Why subscribe?

- Spend less time learning and more time coding with practical eBooks and Videos from over 4,000 industry professionals

- Improve your learning with Skill Plans built especially for you

- Get a free eBook or video every month

- Mapt is fully searchable

- Copy and paste, print, and bookmark content

packt.com

Did you know that Packt offers eBook versions of every book published, with PDF and ePub files available? You can upgrade to the eBook version at `www.packt.com` and, as a print book customer, you are entitled to a discount on the eBook copy. Get in touch with us at `customercare@packtpub.com` for more details.

At `www.packt.com`, you can also read a collection of free technical articles, sign up for a range of free newsletters, and receive exclusive discounts and offers on Packt books and eBooks.

Contributors

About the authors

Priyanka Dive is a DevOps engineer with substantial experience of working in the IT field on various technologies, such as Docker, Kubernetes, Jenkins, AWS, and Azure. She has worked on big data projects as a system and DevOps administrator. She has worked on Salesforce projects and implemented DevOps practices for small and large projects as well. She's a constant learner with a desire to learn anything new, and hence enjoys doing a lot of tech POCs. She is also a technical blogger who loves to write on emerging technologies. She is currently working as a DevOps Engineer Consultant for a US-based firm.

Nagraj Gornalli is a Team Leader at Persistent Systems on Salesforce projects. He has more than eight years' experience in the IT field with different technologies. He has done many certifications' such as Salesforce Certified Administrator, Salesforce Certified Platform Developer, Salesforce Certified Sales Cloud Consultant, Data Integration Specialist, Advanced Apex Specialist, Data Integration Specialist, and cloud certified professional. He started as a trailblazer and is now ranked as a "Ranger" in trailhead.

About the reviewer

Guha Arumugam is a seasoned Salesforce Developer Lead and Technical Consultant with 8 years' expertise in complex implementations. He is a self-taught Salesforce professional with 8X Salesforce certification. He has expertise in all phases of SDLC (discovery and requirement gathering, project design, development/build, testing, and deployment) and Sandbox strategies. He has a solid understanding of Agile and Scrum methodologies.

Guha is also a Salesforce developer evangelist and speaker at various Dreamins across the US. He also leads the Washington DC Salesforce Developer and Salesforce Saturday groups. He is an avid Salesforce blogger and his blog posts have helped many aspiring Salesforce professionals in certifications.

Packt is searching for authors like you

If you're interested in becoming an author for Packt, please visit `authors.packtpub.com` and apply today. We have worked with thousands of developers and tech professionals, just like you, to help them share their insights with the global tech community. You can make a general application, apply for a specific hot topic that we are recruiting an author for, or submit your own idea.

Table of Contents

Preface

Salesforce, with its immense functionalities and features, eases the functioning of an enterprise in various areas, such as sales, marketing, and finance. Deploying Salesforce applications is a tricky business, and it can get quite taxing for administrators and consultants. This book will help you implement DevOps for Salesforce and explore its features. You will learn DevOps principles and techniques for enterprise operations in Salesforce and see how to implement continuous integration and continuous delivery using tools such as Jenkins and Ant scripts. You will also learn how to use the Force.com Migration Tool and Git to achieve versioning in Salesforce.

Who this book is for

If you are a Salesforce developer, consultant, or manager who wants to learn about DevOps tools and set up pipelines for small as well as large Salesforce projects, this book is for you.

What this book covers

Chapter 1, *Salesforce Development and Delivery Process*, gives an overview of the traditional Salesforce development process, including the environments used and how to set up an environment with Eclipse and Force.com IDE. We will also discuss sandboxes and types of sandbox.

Chapter 2, *Applying DevOps to Salesforce Applications*, discusses the need for DevOps in Salesforce projects and what challenges we might face while handling the development and deployment of large Salesforce projects.

Chapter 3, *Deployment in Salesforce*, shows how to deploy Salesforce code from one sandbox to another sandbox, from one sandbox to production, and from one organization to another organization. We will learn about the different types of code deployment and how to use them depending on the type of project.

Chapter 4, *Introduction to the Force.com Migration Tool*, discusses the Force.com Migration Tool and how to set up the tool in your environment. We will also see a sample deployment of metadata to a developer or test sandbox using the Ant Migration Tool.

Chapter 5, *Version Control,* helps you to understand source code versioning systems and their types. We will mainly focus on distributed Git version control. We will also learn about using Git with Salesforce projects and saving Salesforce metadata to Git.

Chapter 6, *Continuous Integration,* shows how to automate backups for Salesforce metadata and push code to the Git repository using Jenkins. We will also learn how to set up our own Jenkins server and configure it to retrieve metadata from our Salesforce sandbox.

Chapter 7, *Continuous Testing,* talks about code quality and continuous testing. We will discuss the tools used in automation testing, such as Selenium and Qualitia. We will also look at a test case in a sample Salesforce application using record and playback in Selenium.

Chapter 8, *Tracking Application Changes and the ROI of Applying DevOps to Salesforce,* discusses the basics of Bugzilla and how to track issues when they are reported by a tester or user. We will also learn how to enhance productivity and measure ROI.

To get the most out of this book

To follow the instructions in this book, you need a Windows system with the following software installed:

- Java
- Eclipse
- Git
- Jenkins
- ANT
- PMD

Download the color images

We also provide a PDF file that has color images of the screenshots/diagrams used in this book. You can download it here: https://www.packtpub.com/sites/default/files/downloads/9781788833349_ColorImages.pdf.

Conventions used

There are a number of text conventions used throughout this book.

CodeInText: Indicates code words in text, database table names, folder names, filenames, file extensions, pathnames, dummy URLs, user input, and Twitter handles. Here is an example: "Enter apex stat into the command panel."

A block of code is set as follows:

```
<?xml version="1.0" encoding="UTF-8"?>
<Package xmlns="http://soap.sforce.com/2006/04/metadata">
    <version>42.0</version>
</Package>
```

When we wish to draw your attention to a particular part of a code block, the relevant lines or items are set in bold:

```
<?xml version="1.0" encoding="UTF-8"?>
<Package xmlns="http://soap.sforce.com/2006/04/metadata">
    <version>42.0</version>
</Package>
```

Any command-line input or output is written as follows:

```
$pmd -d "Source Path" -R apex-ruleset -language apex -f CSV > "Destination
Ptah\ReportName.csv"
```

Bold: Indicates a new term, an important word, or words that you see on screen. For example, words in menus or dialog boxes appear in the text like this. Here is an example: "Enter the **Project name** and **Organization Settings** details for connection."

 Warnings or important notes appear like this.

 Tips and tricks appear like this.

Get in touch

Feedback from our readers is always welcome.

General feedback: Email customercare@packtpub.com and mention the book title in the subject of your message. If you have questions about any aspect of this book, please email us at customercare@packtpub.com.

Errata: Although we have taken every care to ensure the accuracy of our content, mistakes do happen. If you have found a mistake in this book, we would be grateful if you would report this to us. Please visit www.packt.com/submit-errata, selecting your book, clicking on the Errata Submission Form link, and entering the details.

Piracy: If you come across any illegal copies of our works in any form on the Internet, we would be grateful if you would provide us with the location address or website name. Please contact us at copyright@packt.com with a link to the material.

If you are interested in becoming an author: If there is a topic that you have expertise in and you are interested in either writing or contributing to a book, please visit authors.packtpub.com.

Reviews

Please leave a review. Once you have read and used this book, why not leave a review on the site that you purchased it from? Potential readers can then see and use your unbiased opinion to make purchase decisions, we at Packt can understand what you think about our products, and our authors can see your feedback on their book. Thank you!

For more information about Packt, please visit packt.com.

Salesforce Development and Delivery Process

1

Before we jump into the DevOps process for Salesforce or how we can apply DevOps to Salesforce applications, we will first have a look at how typical or traditional Salesforce development is done in organizations.

In this chapter, we will learn about the traditional development process of Salesforce applications. There will be an overview of some Salesforce concepts such as the sandbox, including the different types of sandboxes and how they are differentiated from each other. We will see the development process of the Recruiting application, which is our sample application, and explain Salesforce concepts. We will also discuss the technical challenges we face in the development, deployment, and delivery of Salesforce applications. We will discuss the life of a Salesforce developer without DevOps and the need for DevOps.

In this chapter, we will learn about the following topics:

- The typical Salesforce development process (without DevOps)
- Sandboxes
- Eclipse for Salesforce development
- Business and technical challenges
- The need for DevOps

The typical Salesforce development process (without DevOps)

Salesforce development is different from other stack development platforms. Everything you need to develop an application is available on the cloud. There is no need to install any software. The main drawback of sandbox-based development is that a sandbox does not provide versioning of your code. So, if someone overwrites your code, then you cannot get a previous version of the code. This causes a big mess in large projects where multiple developers are working on the project.

We will start development by creating our own Salesforce Developer Edition account for free. Register with Salesforce for a free-tier account and test it out. Here are some guidelines for new Salesforce users to create their own Salesforce application using `https://developer.salesforce.com/signup`:

1. Log in to your Salesforce account and provide your username and password.
2. Go to setup on top-right corner of your screen. Search for `Apps` in the **Quick Find** box then select **Apps**. You will see the welcome page for apps. On the welcome page, you will see some apps that are enabled for your organization.
3. We want to create a new application. Click on the **New** button. As you are a new user, select **Custom App**. Enter `Recruiting` as the app label name. An app is a collection of tabs that are used to create functionality. Users can switch between apps:

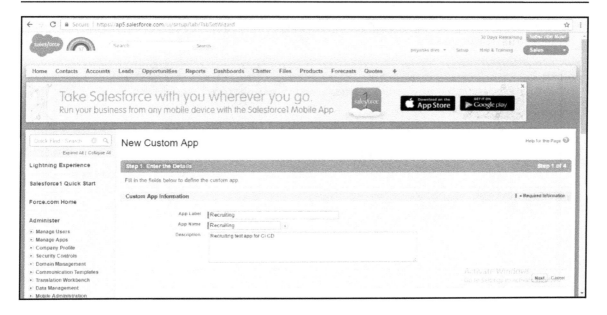

4. On the next screen, you can choose the image that will be used as the application logo. For testing, you can use the default image or upload an image of your choice. You can change it later on.

5. The next screen lets you specify which tabs you want to see on your application. There are already some standard and custom tabs available for you to choose from, or you can create your own custom tabs. For the sample application, you can accept the default and move to the next page. The **Home** tab will be present as the default tab.

6. On the next screen, you need to choose the user profiles that will have access to this application:

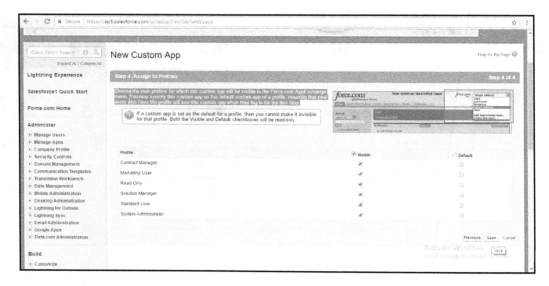

7. Make it visible to the **Standard User** and **System Administrator** profiles.
8. Save it and it's done.

Traditional deployment

There are two ways to deploy code to test in a sandbox or production environment:

- **Change sets**: A change set is used to move changes from a development sandbox to a production environment. Change sets do not contain data. Change sets are best for deploying the same components to multiple organizations. Change sets are good for small deployments, but not preferred for large deployments. The Force.com Migration Tool can be used for large deployments as deployment components can be easily managed.
- **Force.com Migration Tool**: Using the Force.com Migration Tool requires some setup. It is scriptable, so it is used for a multistage release process, where we can easily have scripted retrieval and deployment of components. Repetitive deployments using the parameters can be done. We can retrieve all metadata in the organization, make changes using the editor, and deploy the same subset of components.

Issues with traditional deployment

No versioning is provided in a sandbox environment, so it becomes difficult when multiple developers are working on a project and are not in sync. Keeping track of all changes in project can look like finding a needle in a haystack. Deployment with a change set is not recommended for large projects and creating a change set is not scriptable. So it becomes a repetitive task.

The Force.com Migration Tool is good for large projects, but we do not have versioning, so we cannot revert code to its previous version. Also, we are not able to track changes done by developers.

We have different environments, such as development, test, stage, and production, in almost all technical stacks. In Salesforce, we use a sandbox for development and test environments. Sandboxes come in different types as per our requirement, and we can choose which sandbox to use. Let's look at the different types of sandboxes.

Sandboxes

> *"Sandbox is copy of your production organization that contains the same configuration information or metadata, such as custom objects and fields, process builders, flows, and so on."*

A sandbox is similar to the dev, test, and stage environments in other technology stacks. They are mainly used for the development of Salesforce applications and testing of newly developed features. We do not want to make changes in the production environment directly without testing it thoroughly. So we need these different types of sandboxes; depending on what we can do with them, we can choose which one to use. Some sandboxes only have metadata from production, and some may have both metadata and data in them. Sandboxes also vary in size. Let's see how they differ.

A sandbox is used to develop and test applications. Depending on the type of sandbox you use, it may also include a copy of the data from your production organization. A sandbox is completely isolated from the production organization, so any changes the developers make won't compromise the data, applications, or day-to-day activities of the other users in the production organization. It is ideal for developing complex customizations to minimize risks.

There are various types of sandboxes:

- **Developer**: A Developer sandbox is used for development and testing. It provides a separate environment for coding and testing changes done by developers. According to Salesforce standards, one Developer sandbox should be used by one developer for coding at a time, but it is possible for multiple developers to log in at a time. However, a Developer sandbox does not keep track of changes done in it so there are lots of possibilities that developers may overwrite each other's code. A Developer sandbox has a copy of metadata from production. It does not contain data.

- **Developer Pro**: A Developer Pro sandbox is also used for development and testing purposes, but this sandbox comes with increased storage size. Because of the increased storage size, this sandbox can handle more development workloads and can be used for data load and integration testing.

- **Partial Copy**: A Partial Copy sandbox contains all the metadata from your production organization, and it also contains a sample of the production organization's data, which is defined in the sandbox template while creating a Partial Copy sandbox. As this sandbox contains sample data, it is mainly used for testing purposes. We can use a Partial Copy sandbox for development, testing, and even for training purposes. Most people do not recommend them for load testing purposes.

- **Full**: A Full sandbox is a replica of your production organization. It contains all the metadata and data from the production organization. It contains all data, which includes records, attachments, and so on. You can use sandbox templates to decide which data to copy from the production organization to the Full sandbox, depending on which testing operations you want to perform. A Full sandbox can be used for many purposes and supports load testing, performance testing, and staging. It is difficult to use a Full sandbox for development because it needs a long refresh interval.

Eclipse for Salesforce development

First, we will go through how we can use Eclipse for Salesforce application development. We will start from the very basic steps, such as installing Eclipse and Force.com IDE, followed by configuring Git with Eclipse.

Installing Eclipse Neon with the Force.com IDE plugin

We will start by installing Eclipse on the developer machine. To install Eclipse, you should have a minimum of Java 6 installed. If it is not installed, you can install it from the official website at `https://java.com/en/download/`.

We are going to install Eclipse Neon. Java version 7 is required for Eclipse Neon.

The following are the prerequisites for a development environment for Salesforce:

- Operating systems:
    - Windows 7, 8, or 10
    - macOS 10.7, 10.8, 10.9, 10.10, or 10.11
    - Ubuntu 12.04 LTS or 14.04 LTS
- **Java SE Development Kit (JDK)**, Runtime Environment 8 or later (Java download page).

The installation steps are as follows:

1. Eclipse 4.5 or later is recommended. Go to the download site at `https://www.eclipse.org/downloads/`.
2. Select the appropriate executable package for the operating system you are using.
3. Once the download is complete, you can proceed with Eclipse installation. Double-click on the `.exe` file if you are using Windows.
4. The **Eclipse IDE for Java Developers** distribution is the recommended installer.
5. Choose an installation folder for Eclipse and click on **INSTALL**. It will take some time to install Eclipse.
6. After completing the installation, launch Eclipse. Select the workspace for Eclipse.
7. You will see the welcome page for Eclipse.

Now we have installed Eclipse on our system, we can move forward with the installation of Force.com IDE.

The following are the steps to install Force.com IDE:

1. Launch Eclipse, go to the **Help** option and choose the **Install New Software** option from the drop-down list:

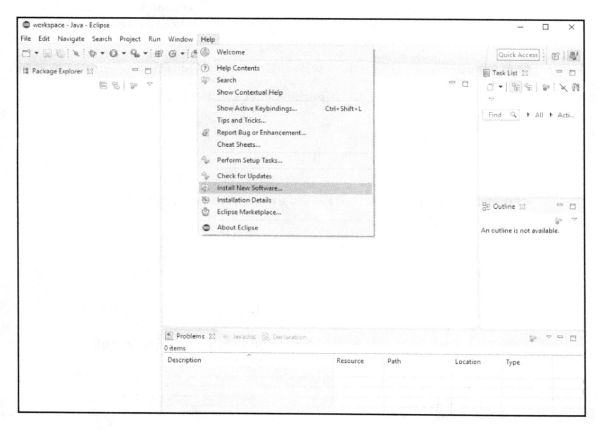

2. Click **Add.**
3. In the **Add Repository** dialog, set the name to Force.com IDE and the location to https://developer.salesforce.com/media/force-ide/eclipse45:

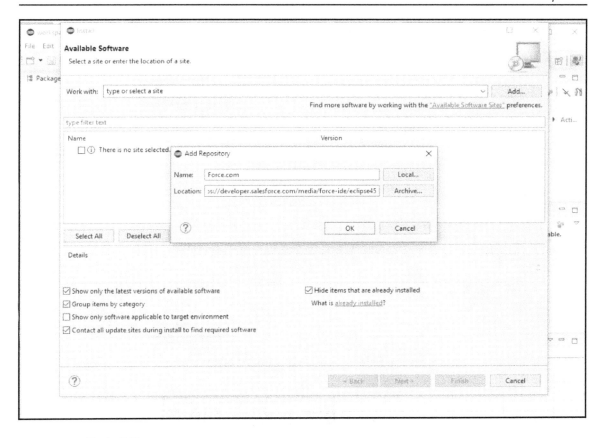

4. Click **OK.**

5. If you are not using Java 8, then deselect **Show only the latest versions of available software**, and it will show an older version of the plugin.

6. Eclipse will show a list of all available plugins. Select the **Force.com IDE** plugin, and then click **Next**.

7. In the **Install Details** dialog, click **Next**.

8. Review the licenses, accept the terms, and click **Finish**.

9. Eclipse starts downloading Force.com IDE and installs it and other required dependencies. Once the installation is completed, you need to restart Eclipse to reflect the changes. Click **Yes**.

10. When Eclipse restarts, select **Window** | **Open Perspective** | **Other**. Select **Force.com** and then click **OK**:

We are done with setting up the Salesforce development environment in Eclipse.

Configuring a Force.com project in Eclipse

We have a Salesforce application, and we want Salesforce code in the local workspace we just created using Force.com IDE:

1. Right-click on the **Package Explorer** area, then choose **New** and select **Force.com Project**:

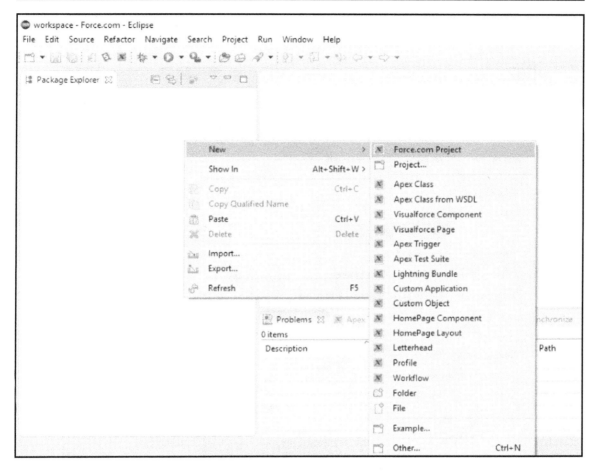

2. Create a new Force.com project. You need to provide details about your project. Enter the **Project name** and **Organization Settings** details for connection:

   • **Username**: Provide a username and append the sandbox name to it.

   • **Password**: Provide a password for the given username.

   • **Security Token**: You need to provide a security token for the sandbox.

- **Environment:** Choose the environment you are using, such as sandbox or Production Edition:

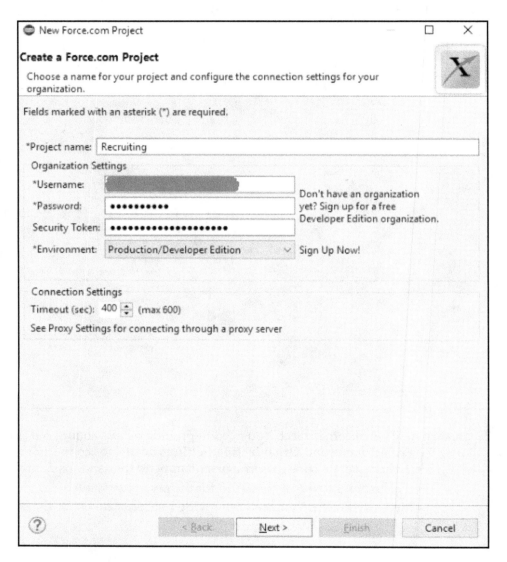

3. Once you have filled in all the details, click **Next**.

We will get all the code in Eclipse from Salesforce. Now, whatever changes a developer makes in Eclipse will be in sync with the sandbox being used.

Technical and business challenges

Following traditional methods for the deployment of Salesforce projects is time-consuming. Also, the major problem is with versioning of code, which causes issues in every environment. A particular feature may run perfectly in a Developer sandbox, but we might face issues in production. Tracking every change done by developers and administrators is very difficult, so the miscommunication between teams can result in failed deployments or delay in product delivery.

We can consider scenario where a particular feature needs to be launched as soon as possible and we are facing deployment issues. We may not able to resolve it in time and this will impact on our customers and business as well. We will face challenges such as the following:

- Failed deployments
- Unable to track issues
- No code coverage
- Failed test cases

We need to streamline all these issues and have one solution which will solve almost all problems; here, DevOps comes into the picture!!

DevOps for Salesforce?

Yes, we can apply DevOps practice to Salesforce projects and achieve continuous integration and deployment, and continuous testing for Salesforce projects as well. In DevOps, we have a rich toolset that can also be used for Salesforce projects.

Let's try to cover this step by step. The first and most important consideration is how we can achieve versioning in Salesforce where the Salesforce sandbox itself doesn't keep versions of code stored. A Salesforce sandbox stores only a minimal amount of information about changes, such as which user made the previous change and its timestamp. Obviously, this information is not enough to achieve full versioning. We can use a very popular source code management tool, Git for Salesforce projects, where the sandbox will be in sync with the Eclipse workspace and Git repository.

Salesforce provides a very useful tool for migration of metadata from a local repository to a sandbox, which is the Force.com Migration Tool. The Force.com Migration Tool is an Ant-based tool for moving metadata from a sandbox to local repositories. With the Force.com Migration Tool, we can perform operations such as retrieving metadata from a sandbox and deploying metadata to a sandbox.

Using this Force.com Migration Tool with Jenkins, we can build our continuous integration jobs. Jenkins is an automation server that allows us to automate tasks such as building, testing, and deploying software on a particular environment. Jenkins is written in Java programming language and allows us to create continuous integration jobs. In later chapters, we will see how to use the Force.com Migration Tool with Jenkins and automate continuous integration tasks in Salesforce projects.

Finding issues can be like finding a needle in haystack. We need to track issues in our project. There are many applications present that we can use in our projects, such as Bug Tracker and Jira. This helps us to get an idea about issues in our project and in which environment they are present; also, it helps us be on track and stay updated. We will see some of these applications in detail in later chapters. We will also see how we can integrate these tools and have a CI-CD pipeline for Salesforce projects.

Achieving continuous testing with Salesforce is possible with the help of tools such as Selenium and Qualitia. Selenium is a testing framework that is used to test web applications. Qualitia is a scriptless automation tool that helps to create test cases without writing scripts/code.

Do you still have doubts about applying DevOps to Salesforce? The answer can be positive or negative, but, wait, do not mark it as your final answer because you have still to read the following chapters, where we will try to provide a clearer idea about using DevOps tools for Salesforce projects. Also, we will cover some examples and real-time scenarios about DevOps and Salesforce, so stay tuned!

Summary

In this chapter, we got an overview of the traditional Salesforce development process, which environments are used for Salesforce development, and how we can set up a Salesforce development environment with Eclipse and Force.com IDE. Also we looked into sandboxes and the types of sandboxes used in Salesforce projects, and how they differ from each other.

We also got some information about traditional deployment methods used for Salesforce projects, such as change sets and the Force.com Migration Tool and discussed which method is suitable for small and large projects. We also looked into technical and business challenges in Salesforce.

In the next chapter, we will see how we can apply DevOps for Salesforce projects. We will compare other technical stacks with Salesforce and see how applying DevOps to Salesforce is different than DevOps in other technical stacks. We will also discuss various ways to apply DevOps to Salesforce.

2
Applying DevOps to Salesforce Applications

In the previous chapter, we learned some basics about the Salesforce development process, what a sandbox is, the different types of sandbox, and how to choose a sandbox according to our needs. We developed our own recruiting application using Salesforce, followed by learning the traditional ways used for Salesforce deployment. We also had a look at the issues we face during traditional deployments of Salesforce applications. We learned Salesforce development setup with Eclipse. We discussed applying DevOps to Salesforce applications.

In this chapter, we will discuss why there is a need for DevOps in Salesforce applications. We will also discuss the problems we face while working on big projects that involve large numbers of developers, testers, and so on. We will try to get a clear idea about how applying DevOps for Salesforce is different from other tech stacks such as simple Java application stacks. We will differentiate between the development process involved in Salesforce applications and that of other tech stacks such as Java, PHP, Ruby, and so on. We will also see in detail the DevOps process in Java applications to get a clearer idea about the DevOps continuous integration and delivery process using DevOps tools. We will go through a step-by-step process to set up a simple continuous integration pipeline with Jenkins and Git. We will also learn how to install required plugins, configure the Maven plugin in Jenkins, and how to add a Jenkins webhook URL in a GitHub project; we'll also implement continuous deployment using the Jenkins plugin. Finally, we will see how we can deploy our code whenever any changes are pushed to GitHub.

In this chapter, we will learn about the following topics:

- The need for a DevOps process in Salesforce development.
- The differences between DevOps for Salesforce and DevOps for other tech stacks. For example, the typical DevOps process for a Java development stack

The need for a DevOps process in Salesforce development

As discussed in the previous chapter, we can apply DevOps practices in Salesforce projects to achieve faster delivery of applications. The question arises, *Why do we need DevOps?*

Let's discuss some normal development practices in Salesforce projects. In Salesforce, everything is on the cloud, you just need a browser and internet connection to start developing your application. But as the development team grows, the complexities of building different features and deploying them in a production environment also become difficult. Although we can use different types of sandbox according to our need, managing the deployment process is still a time-consuming task.

Given that multiple developers are working on different features in different sandbox environments, we need to cherry-pick some features from those environments and deploy them to a **user acceptance testing** (**UAT**) environment. This process is error-prone as it involves human interaction at various phases. Also we don't have any system for version control to manage changes done by developers.

Let's assume that somehow we managed to work with multiple developers with multiple sandbox environments and without managing the source code (that is just a hypothetical case but consider it is possible). What about testing new features in your application, and more importantly ensuring that nothing breaks in the previous application? Achieving this with manual testing would require a large number of testers and still we can't ensure that we have tested each and every feature right from login to some complex feature we just introduced in our application.

Why make such a mess when we can achieve more a streamlined delivery with the help of DevOps? DevOps reduces the time of delivery and makes the process less prone to errors; tracking applications becomes easier with a different set of open-source tools. We can improve the Salesforce application development process by integrating it with a DevOps toolset such as Git to maintain our source code version. We can integrate Jenkins for the deployment of Salesforce applications. We will see how to do this in more detail in Chapter 6, *Continuous Integration*.

DevOps helps applications in other stacks to get more productive and follow a faster delivery process. We can achieve fast delivery in Salesforce projects with some modifications to the development and delivery processes. DevOps will impact everyone who is involved in Salesforce application development, testing, and deployment directly or indirectly, along with other end users.

The differences between DevOps for Salesforce and other tech stacks

Applying DevOps in Salesforce is different from other environments; let's look at this step by step.

First, we will talk about the development process. Salesforce development is easy to start with because you don't need any installations and extra setup on your development machines. All you need is an internet connection and a browser supported by Salesforce platforms, such as Internet Explorer, Google Chrome, Safari, and so on. As we demonstrated in the previous chapter, a sample application in Salesforce is easy to develop with some clicks as Salesforce provides some existing applications and tabs for you to reuse. We can create some custom tabs in our application according to our requirements. When it comes to other tech stacks such as Java, to get started with development we need to install Java on our machines and set up some environment variables.

In tech stacks such as Java, JavaScript, PHP, and Ruby, the most common thing is using version control systems such as Git, CVS, SVN, and so on, which help to keep track of application changes done by each developer. Version control systems make it possible for multiple developers to work on a single project or module without overwriting each other's changes. In some situations, such as when something goes wrong and unfortunately we need to roll back updates, version control is very useful.

When we have a small team of one or two developers working on a Salesforce application, we may not need to use version control. But when it comes to teams with multiple developers working on different sandboxes, developing different features releasing at different timelines or sprints, it becomes necessary to have version control for a streamlined development and delivery process.

There are some ways to deploy changes to Salesforce production organizations, such as using Change Set, Eclipse, and Ant. For deployment using Change Set, you need to connect organizations using Deployment Connection. Eclipse uses metadata for deployment and it is mostly used by developers. Using Ant for deployment, we can perform file-based deployment to production organizations.

Example – the typical DevOps process for a Java development stack

The prerequisites are as follows:

- Java version 1.6 or above
- Apache Maven 3.5.2
- Jenkins server

 Note: Use latest version of software available. In future, the previous versions may not be compatible.

If you haven't already installed Java, you can download it from the official website: `https://java.com/en/download/`.

Use the following commands for this sample CI/CD application. I will be using an Ubuntu 16.04 instance for setup. So let's start by installing Java.

Log in to your Ubuntu server machine as a normal user. We need a user with `sudo` access for installing packages on the machine. I will be using the Ubuntu username for this example:

```
# sudo apt-get update
# sudo apt-get install default-jdk
```

The previous commands will install Java version 8 on the machine. Verify this with the following command:

 Note: The same setup should work if the Java version is incremented to a stable version.

```
$java -version
openjdk version "1.8.0_151"
OpenJDK Runtime Environment (build 1.8.0_151-8u151-b12-0ubuntu0.16.04.2-b12)
OpenJDK 64-Bit Server VM (build 25.151-b12, mixed mode)
```

Now, we have Java in place, so we will move on to the installation of Maven. The installation steps are as follows:

1. Download Maven from the official website:

```
$wget
http://www-eu.apache.org/dist/maven/maven-3/3.5.2/binaries/apache-m
aven-3.5.2-bin.tar.gz
```

2. Extract the package using the following:

```
$tar -xvf apache-maven-3.5.2-bin.tar.gz
```

3. We need to set up environment variables. Add a path to `.bashrc`:

```
$export M2_HOME=/home/ubuntu/apache-maven-3.5.2
$export PATH=${M2_HOME}/bin:${PATH}
$source ~/.bashrc
```

4. Verify whether Maven was installed on your machine:

```
$ mvn -v
Apache Maven 3.5.2 (138edd61fd100ec658bfa2d307c43b76940a5d7d;
2017-10-18T07:58:13Z)
Maven home: /home/ubuntu/apache-maven-3.5.2
Java version: 1.8.0_151, vendor: Oracle Corporation
Java home: /usr/lib/jvm/java-8-openjdk-amd64/jre
Default locale: en_US, platform encoding: ANSI_X3.4-1968
OS name: "linux", version: "4.4.0-1049-aws", arch: "amd64", family:
"unix"
```

We will create a project in Maven. Here we will be using the official Maven example *Maven in 5 Minutes*. You will find a link in the **References** section.

Let's move on to creating a sample project in Maven:

```
$mvn archetype:generate -DgroupId=com.mycompany.app -DartifactId=my-app -
DarchetypeArtifactId=maven-archetype-quickstart -DinteractiveMode=false
```

It will take some time to download dependencies. After completing execution of command, it will create a directory with value passed to `DartifactId` that is `my-app`.

In this example, `src/main/java` contains source code, `src/test/java` has test code, and `pom.xml` contains all information required to build the project.

The following is the source code we have from the sample app:

```
cat src/main/java/com/mycompany/app/App.java
package com.mycompany.app;
/**
 * Hello world!
 *
 */
public class App
{
    public static void main( String[] args )
    {
        System.out.println( "Hello World!" );
    }
}
```

Now we will build our sample project:

```
#mvn package
```

This will compile the project and create a JAR in the target folder as my-app-1.0-SNAPSHOT.jar.

Test the JAR with the following command:

```
#java -cp target/my-app-1.0-SNAPSHOT.jar com.mycompany.app.App
```

We get the following output:

```
Hello World!
```

So, we got our sample application running but what if we have many developers working on the project? We need a version control tool and some standard procedure for deploying this project to the server environment. For this, we will follow our sample DevOps pipeline with Git and Jenkins.

Git is a version control tool that helps us to track changes in our source code and coordinate our work with different developments. It is the most commonly used version control tool nowadays. We will have a look at Git in depth in Chapter 5, *Version Control*. For this sample pipeline, we can use a GitHub account.

Create a repository on GitHub and push sample code to this repository:

```
$cd my-app
$Git init
$Git add .
$Git commit -m "first commit"
```

```
$Git remote add origin https://Github.com/priyankadive/devops-sample.Git
$Git push -u origin master
```

Now that we have our version control ready, we will move on to the next step in using a continuous integration and continuous delivery process using Jenkins.

Jenkins is an open-source tool written in the Java programming language. It is used to automate continuous integration and continuous delivery jobs. We will see Jenkins in detail in `Chapter 6`, *Continuous Integration*.

Let's get started with Jenkins:

1. Install Jenkins. I have installed Jenkins on an Ubuntu server.
2. Log in to the Jenkins server.
3. Install the required Jenkins plugins on the Jenkins server using the following process.
4. Go to **Manage Jenkins | GitHub Plugin** and search for `maven plugin`.
5. Install the Maven plugin in Jenkins if it was not installed while setting up Jenkins. You need to configure Maven in Jenkins **Global Tool Configuration** as we have already installed it.

Configuring Maven in the Jenkins server

Go to **Manage Jenkins | Global Tool Configuration**.

We have already installed Maven on our machine. So enter a name for the Maven installation and the `M2_HOME` path as follows:

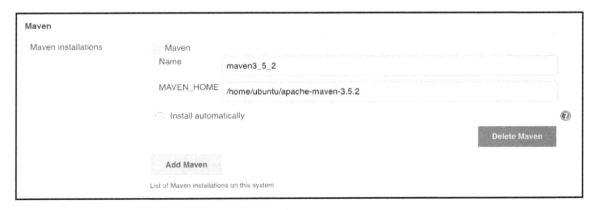

Let's configure our Jenkins job to build our sample project:

1. Click on **create new jobs**:

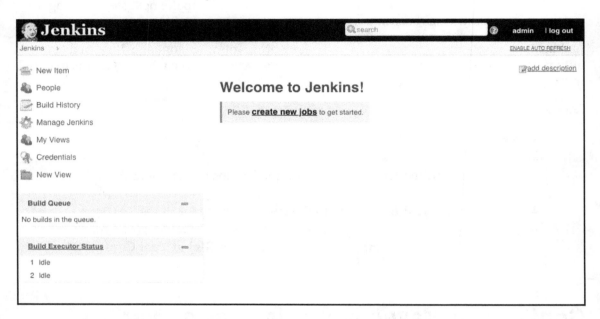

2. Create a Jenkins job with the Maven plugin. Provide the job name `devops-ci-cd` (you can choose another project name, if you want):

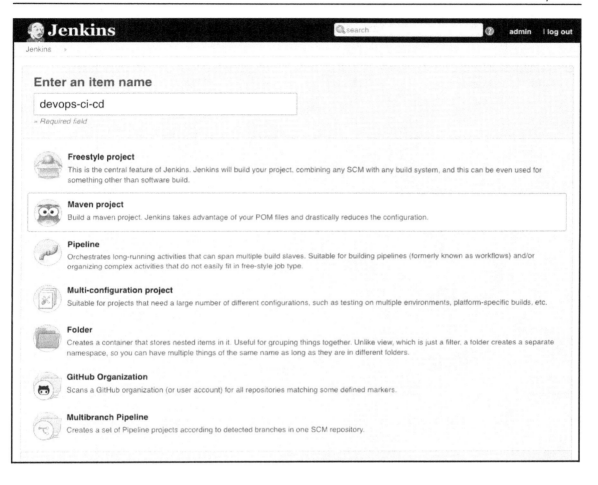

Jenkins

search · admin · I log out

Jenkins »

Enter an item name

devops-ci-cd

» *Required field*

Freestyle project
This is the central feature of Jenkins. Jenkins will build your project, combining any SCM with any build system, and this can be even used for something other than software build.

Maven project
Build a maven project. Jenkins takes advantage of your POM files and drastically reduces the configuration.

Pipeline
Orchestrates long-running activities that can span multiple build slaves. Suitable for building pipelines (formerly known as workflows) and/or organizing complex activities that do not easily fit in free-style job type.

Multi-configuration project
Suitable for projects that need a large number of different configurations, such as testing on multiple environments, platform-specific builds, etc.

Folder
Creates a container that stores nested items in it. Useful for grouping things together. Unlike view, which is just a filter, a folder creates a separate namespace, so you can have multiple things of the same name as long as they are in different folders.

GitHub Organization
Scans a GitHub organization (or user account) for all repositories matching some defined markers.

Multibranch Pipeline
Creates a set of Pipeline projects according to detected branches in one SCM repository.

3. In the **Source Code Management** section, provide the Git URL of your project. Provide credentials to clone the repository in Jenkins:

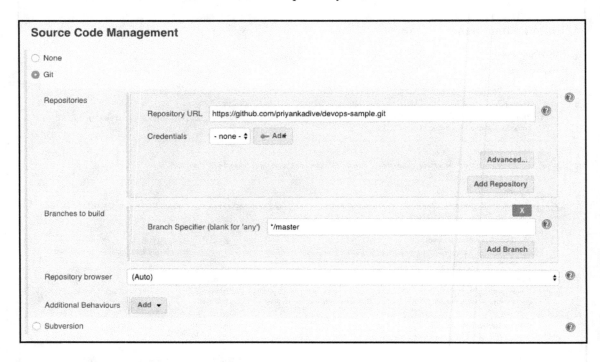

4. Choose **GitHub hook trigger for GitScm polling** in **Build Triggers**. If Jenkins receives a PUSH GitHub webhook from the preceding repository, it will trigger this job:

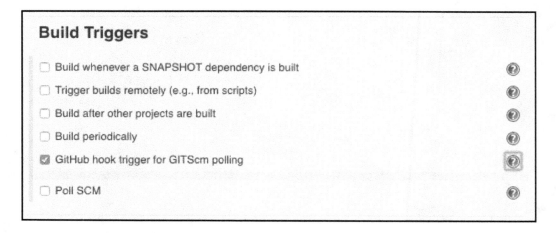

5. Provide a path to root `pom.xml`. It will be a relative path to the module root. In **Build**, add **Root POM** as `pom.xml` and **Goals and options** as `package`:

6. Save your work and click on **Build now**.

This will create `my-app-1.0-SNAPSHOT.jar` in the `/var/lib/Jenkins/workspace/target` folder. You can check the console logs while the project build is in progress.

Once the JAR is successfully built, you can see the console logs as shown in the following screenshot:

```
[INFO] Building jar: /var/lib/jenkins/workspace/devops-ci-cd/target/my-app-1.0-SNAPSHOT.jar
[INFO] ------------------------------------------------------------------------
[INFO] BUILD SUCCESS
[INFO] ------------------------------------------------------------------------
[INFO] Total time: 15.739 s
[INFO] Finished at: 2018-02-25T10:06:08Z
[INFO] Final Memory: 20M/49M
[INFO] ------------------------------------------------------------------------
[JENKINS] Archiving /var/lib/jenkins/workspace/devops-ci-cd/pom.xml to com.mycompany.app/my-app/1.0-SNAPSHOT/my-app-1.0-SNAPSHOT.pom
[JENKINS] Archiving /var/lib/jenkins/workspace/devops-ci-cd/target/my-app-1.0-SNAPSHOT.jar to com.mycompany.app/my-app/1.0-
SNAPSHOT/my-app-1.0-SNAPSHOT.jar
channel stopped
Finished: SUCCESS
```

We have completed a continuous integration job successfully. Now, we need to add the Jenkins webhook URL in the GitHub settings to trigger a Jenkins build whenever someone pushes code to our GitHub project.

Adding a Jenkins webhook URL in a GitHub project

To add a Jenkins webhook URL, you need to perform the following steps:

1. Grab your GitHub webhook URL from **Manage Jenkins | Configure System | GitHub Web Hook Section**.

   Example URL: `https://<your-domain-name or IP address>/web-hook/`

2. Go to **GitHub | Choose your project**. Go to **Settings** and select **Integrations and Services**. Click on **Add service** and search for `Jenkins`. As a result, you will see two service: Jenkins (Git plugin) and Jenkins (GitHub plugin). Choose one according to your project. We are going for **Jenkins (GitHub plugin)**:

3. Add your Jenkins webhook URL and click on **Add service**:

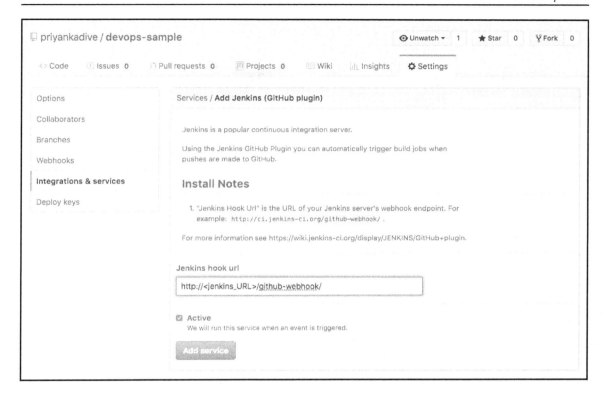

4. Verify that the hook is working by clicking on **Test service**. It will send our test payload to the Jenkins server. If everything is working fine, then we will see a green check mark before the Jenkins webhook:

To test your continuous integration pipeline, add some changes in the README file we created. Push changes to GitHub.

5. In Jenkins, you can see the "devops-ci-cd" build is automatically started as shown in the following screenshot:

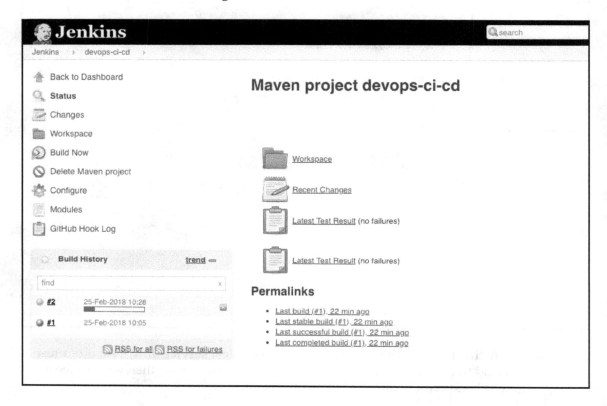

Continuous deployment

We have completed the continuous integration step. When source code is updated in a GitHub project, our Jenkins server will build a `.jar` file. We need to deploy the updated code to a remote server. SSH is secure shell protocol widely used to securely log in to remote systems. In this sample application, we will be using the Publish Over SSH plugin. It is used to send build artifacts and execute commands on remote server using the SSH protocol.

Installing the Publish Over SSH plugin in a Jenkins server

Now, we will edit the Jenkins job which we created earlier. As the output of the continuous integration step, we get `my-app-1.0-SNAPSHOT.jar` created in our Jenkins workspace. To deploy this JAR on our test server, we are going to use a simple Jenkins plugin called Publish Over SSH. This plugin allows us to transfer files to a remote server and run commands as well. First we need to set up an SSH private key on the **Manage Jenkins** page. Go to **Manage Jenkins | Configure System** and provide the following information:

- **Passphrase**: Provide a passphrase for the key (leave it blank if not encrypted)
- **Path to key**: The path to the key can be absolute, or relative to `$JENKINS_HOME`
- **Key**: If the key is not present on Jenkins server then you can copy and paste it in this field
- Add **SSH Server** details such as **Username**, **Hostname**, and **Remote Directory**:

Now go to our previous Jenkins job and choose the **Run only if build succeeds** option from **Post Steps** so that if the build is successful then only the post steps will be executed.

From the **Add post-build step** drop-down list, select the **Send files or execute commands over SSH** option:

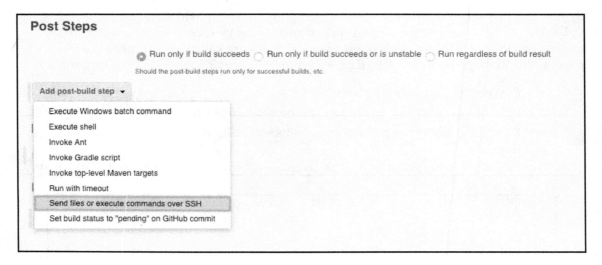

Add the following configuration to copy the JAR to the test server and run the command to start it:

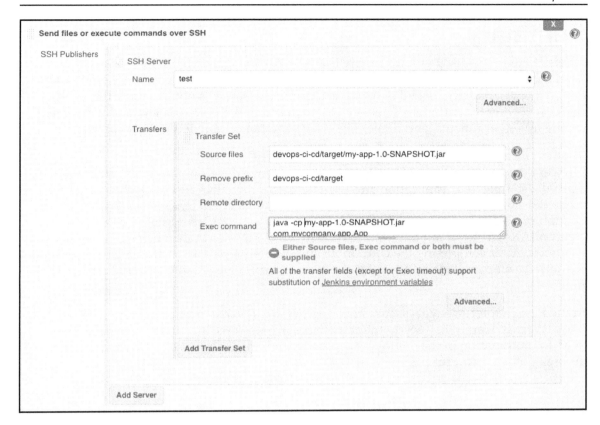

The command to deploy `Hello world!` is as follows:

```
#java -cp target/my-app-1.0-SNAPSHOT.jar com.mycompany.app.App
```

We have completed the continuous integration and Continuous Deployment process for our sample Java application using Maven and Jenkins. So, whenever any developer commits code to Git, the Jenkins job will be triggered, which will execute the build step to create a JAR and deploy it to the test server, if the build is successful. We can add one more step where we can execute automated test cases on the deployed application and get the results of our new changes.

Summary

In this chapter, we discussed why there is a need for DevOps in Salesforce projects, and what challenges we might face while handling large Salesforce project developments and deployments. Also, we looked at why DevOps for Salesforce is not like any other tech stacks and what the differences between them are from the point of view of development, setting up environments, and deploying changes to the production environment in Salesforce and other stacks.

We went through the typical DevOps process for a Java development stack, where we created a sample Java application and used Git version-control and track changes done while developing the application. We worked on how to add a Jenkins webhook URL in a GitHub project. We set up a sample Jenkins job where we added a Maven build step to create a JAR whenever anyone pushes code to the Git master branch using a Jenkins webhook. After completing the continuous integration step for our sample Java application, we added a step in the Jenkins job for continuous deployment using the Publish Over SSH plugin.

In the next chapter, we will discuss how deployment is done in Salesforce in traditional ways. We will learn what deployment methods in Salesforce are, and discuss why there is a need for automation in the deployment process and how Salesforce deployments can be automated using Ant scripts.

References

Maven in 5 Minutes: `https://maven.apache.org/guides/getting-started/maven-in-five-minutes.html`

3
Deployment in Salesforce

In the previous chapter, we discussed the need for DevOps in Salesforce application deployment, and different scenarios where DevOps can make it easy for a large number of developers to work on the same project. We saw that DevOps can give us streamlined delivery, helping us track application issues with open source tools. We also took a look at how Salesforce is different from other technical stacks. We went through the process of setting up DevOps for the Java development stack using Git and Jenkins.

In this chapter, we are going to discuss how to deploy Salesforce code from one sandbox to another sandbox, or from a sandbox to production, in a transitional way. There are various ways to deploy code, such as using Change Sets or a migration tool.

In this chapter, we will learn about the following topics:

- What is deployment with reference to DevOps?
- Deployment from sandbox to sandbox and sandbox organization
- Deployment using Change Sets
- Deployment using a migration tool
- Deployment using the Force.com IDE
- Deployment using Visual Studio Code with Salesforce DX plugins
- Deployment using third-party tools that use the Metadata API or the Tooling API

Let's start by looking at deployment in Salesforce.

What is deployment with reference to DevOps?

Successful deployment of code changes to a production environment involves many tasks, such as unit testing, integration testing, configuration changes, avoiding downtime, taking a backup of the existing environment to avoid data loss in the event of failed deployment, provisioning to revert changes quickly, and so on. In DevOps, with the help of many deployment, configuration management, backup, and restore tools, it is easy to perform fast, zero-downtime deployments.

In DevOps, continuous deployment is the process of deploying every change from a development environment to a production environment, where every change goes through the pipeline of continuous integration, with testing happening automatically. This process allows us to deliver new features and bug fixes to a production environment more quickly.

As every change goes through the DevOps pipeline, everything is tracked. For example, say we wanted to deploy Java application code from a development to a production environment, as we saw in Chapter 2, *Applying DevOps to a Salesforce Application*. Code changes done by developers would be pushed to Git (a version control system), which automatically triggers a Jenkins job for build JAR files and deploy them to a test environment. We could go on adding continuous testing stages to a build job where we run test cases and, depending on the result of the test case, the build would be promoted to the next environment stage and then on to production.

The deployment process in Salesforce is different to deployment in other stacks. We will discuss what types of deployment there are in Salesforce and the differences between them, with some example scenarios. We will also learn how many ways there are to deploy a project in Salesforce and which one is best.

Deployment in Salesforce

There are many different ways to deploy Salesforce in production. Salesforce deployment involves simply moving Salesforce metadata to production.

There are three ways to move metadata to production:

- From a sandbox to a Production Org
- From one Production Org to another Production Org
- From a developer org to a Production Org

There are various methods to achieve Salesforce metadata deployment:

- Change Sets
- The Ant Migration Tool
- The Force.com IDE
- Third-party tools that use the Metadata API or the Tooling API
- The SOAP API
- Visual Studio Code with Salesforce DX plugins

Change Sets

To use a Change Set, a sandbox must be connected to a Production Organization. In the previous chapter, we discussed creating a sandbox and creating a connection between the sandbox and production organization. This is the traditional and most simple way to send configuration and metadata changes from one sandbox to another or from one sandbox to a Production Organization.

There are two different types of Change Set. Go to **Setup** and search with the `Change Set` keyword.

The two types of Change Set are inbound Change Sets and Outbound Change Sets:

- **Outbound Change Sets**: Outbound Change Sets need to be created in the source sandbox. Typically, we create an Outbound Change Set in a sandbox and deploy it to the Production Organization. We might choose to migrate changes from the sandbox to the Production Organization, from the Production Organization to the sandbox, or from sandbox to sandbox. You need to make changes in the source sandbox and upload those changes to the destination sandbox or Production Organization.
- **Inbound Change Sets**: Inbound Change Sets are automatically visible in the destination sandbox or Production Organization, once the outbound sandbox has been uploaded successfully.

Deployment connections

Before creating Change Sets in a sandbox or other organization, we need to authorize a deployment connection in the organization. Go to **Setup** and search with the `Deployment` keyword:

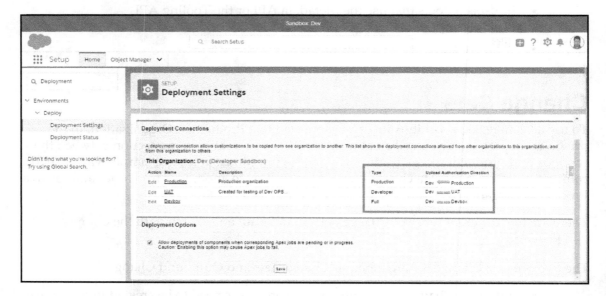

The Setup page

Deployment using Change Sets

There are four steps to deployment using Change Sets. They are as follows:

1. Creating deployment connections
2. Creating Outbound Change Sets
3. Validating inbound Change Sets
4. Using **Quick Deploy** to deploy Change Sets

We will discuss these steps in the following sections.

Creating deployment connections

First, go to **Setup** and search with the `deployment` keyword:

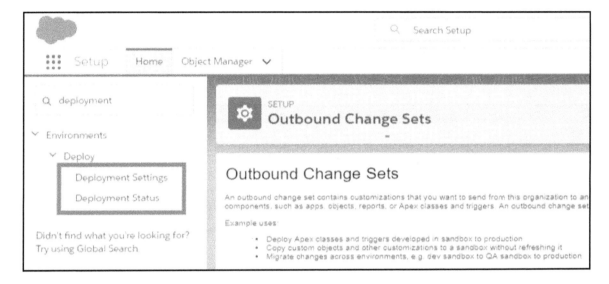

Select **Deployment Settings**:

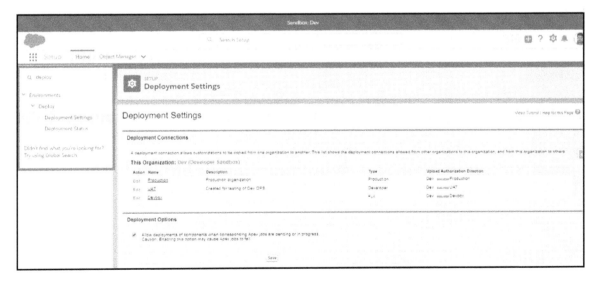

Selecting Deployment Settings

Here we can find a list of the sandboxes and their connection statuses.

There are three different types of symbol:

- Green colored arrow pointing to the right
- Green colored arrow pointing to the left and right
- Red colored broken arrow

Select **Edit** to modify inbound changes:

Modifying inbound changes

There is a checkbox labeled **Allow Inbound Changes.** This is for the connected organization that is authorized to deploy Change Sets to our organization. We need to select this checkbox to establish the connection:

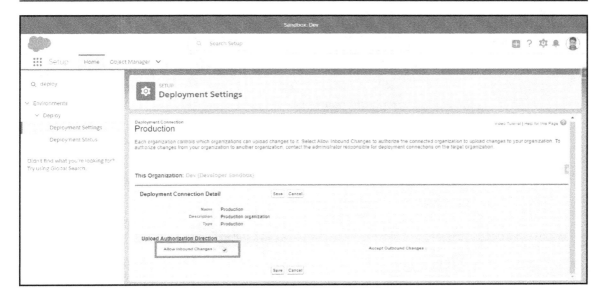

Allowing Inbound Changes

There is a checkbox labeled **Accept Outbound Changes**. This is a read-only field—you cannot edit this field from here. This value is automatically selected if the connected organization has selected the **Allow Inbound Changes** checkbox:

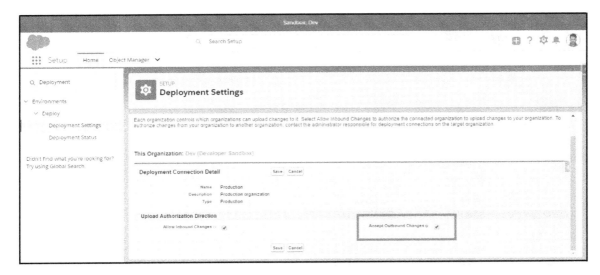

Allowing Outbound Changes

Now click on the **Save** button to create the connection:

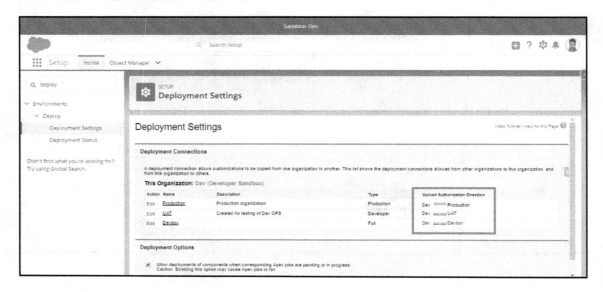

Creating Outbound Change Sets

Go to **Setup** and search with the outbound keyword:

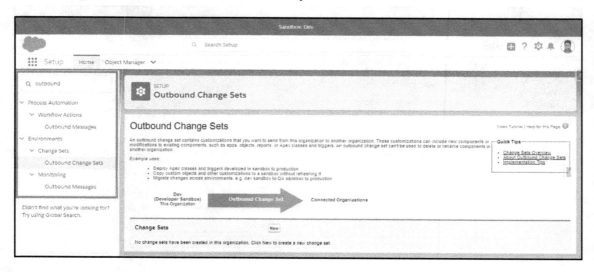

Searching with outbound keyword

An Outbound Change Set contains customization that you want to send from this organization to another organization. This customization could include new components or modifications to existing components, such as apps, objects, reports, or Apex classes and triggers. An Outbound Change Set can't be used to delete or rename components in another organization.

To create a new **Outbound Change Set**, hit the **New** button.

Add the name of the Change Set, which is mandatory, and enter its description:

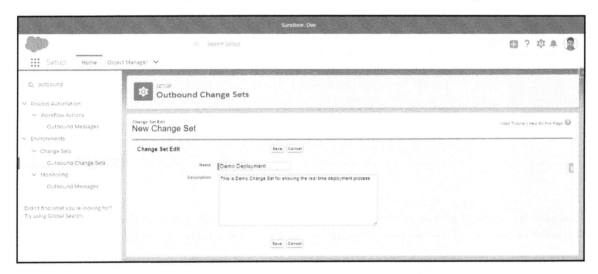

Creating Outbound Change Set

Hit the **Save** button to create the Outbound Change Set.

A Change Set contains customization for components such as apps, objects, reports, and email templates. You can use Change Sets to move customizations from one organization to another.

After a Change Set has been uploaded, its components aren't refreshed and you can't add or remove components. To refresh the source of components and modify the component list, clone the Change Set.

Click on **Add** to include Salesforce components in your Change Set:

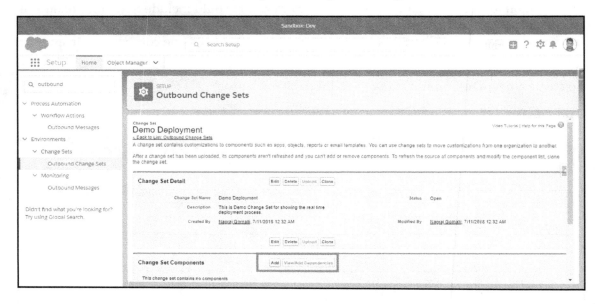

Adding Salesforce components

You will see a list of all the Salesforce components, from which you can choose the component you want to add and its type:

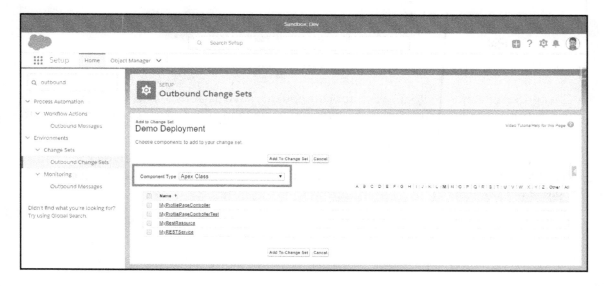

Select the components that need to move to the Production Organization:

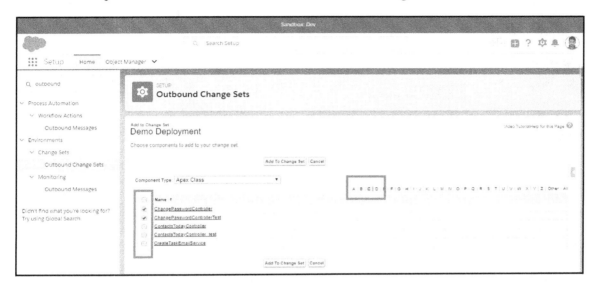

Click on **Add to Change Set**.

We can remove components if they've been added by mistake. You do so by clicking on the **Remove** link:

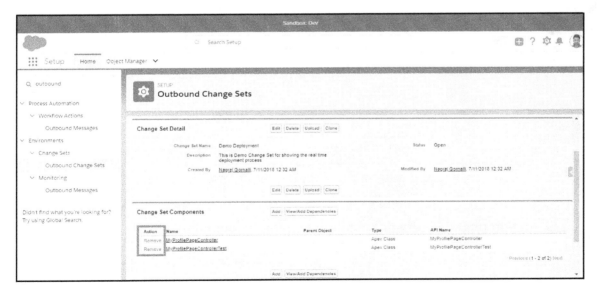

Removing components

Now hit the **Upload** button to upload the Change Set:

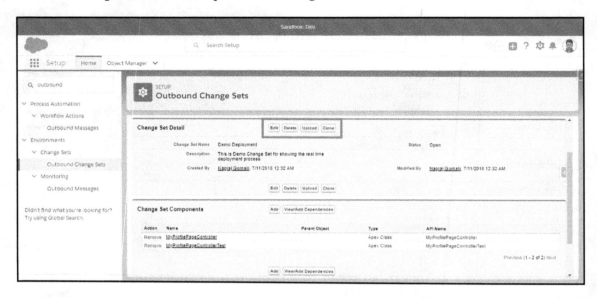

Options for Change Set

Once you upload this Change Set, you won't be able to edit it or recall it from the target organization:

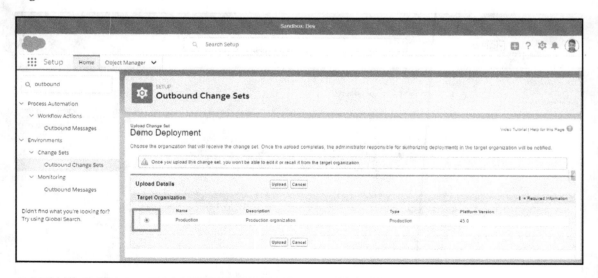

Upload confirmation message

Select the organization you want to send the Change Set to and then click **Upload**. You will get a confirmation message, as shown in the following screenshot:

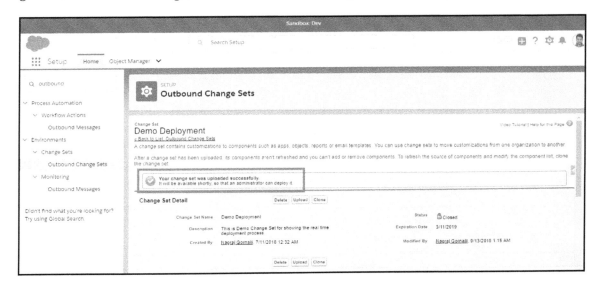

Validating Inbound Change Sets

Go to **Setup** and search with the `inbound` keyword:

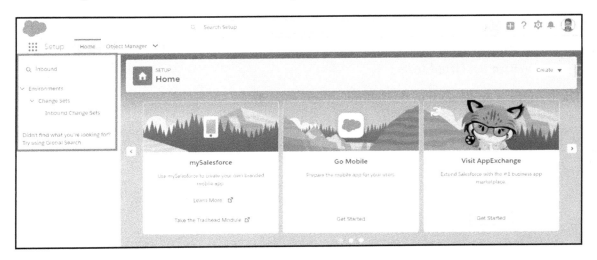

Searching with inbound keyword

Then select **Inbound Change Sets** and click a Change Set name to see its details:

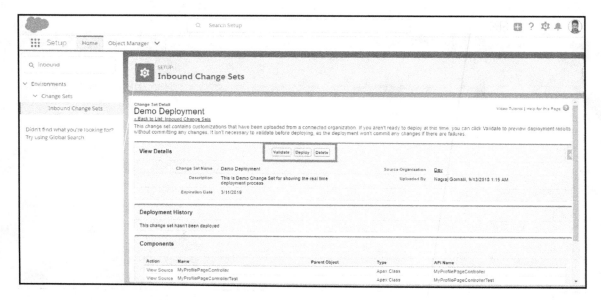

There are three options: **Validate**, **Deploy**, and **Delete**. Click on **Validate** to validate a Change Set without deploying changes.

There are four options for validating a Change Set:

- **Default**
- **Run local tests**
- **Run all tests**
- **Run specified tests**

These options are shown in the following screenshot:

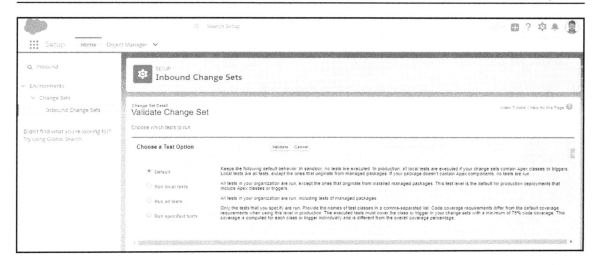

Salesforce recommends that you select the **Run Specified Tests** option. In the following screen we need to add specific test classes:

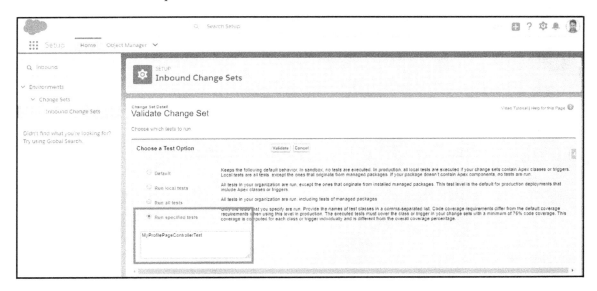

Click **Validate** to validate the Change Set on the Production Organization:

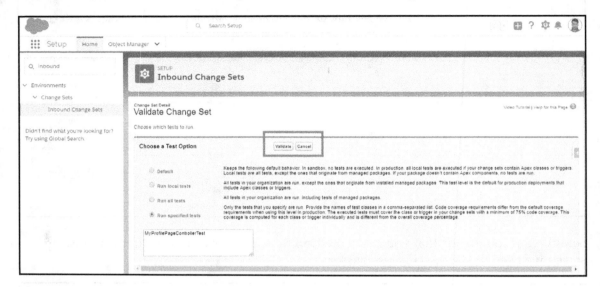

On the confirmation prompt, click on **OK**:

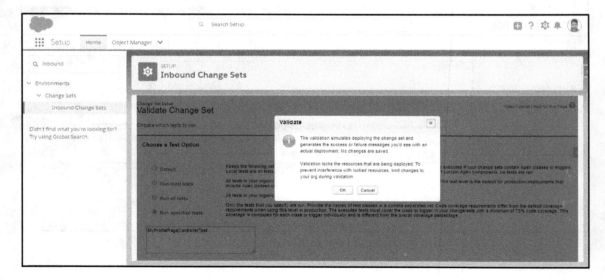

Using Quick Deploy to deploy Change Sets

To track validation progress, click on **Deployment Status**:

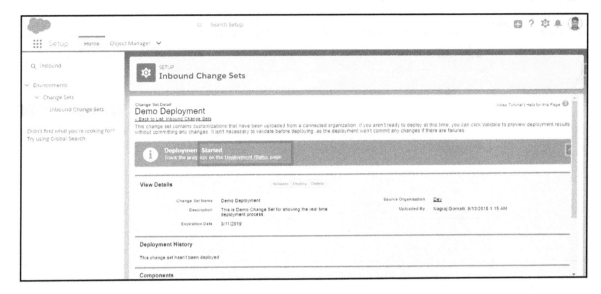

We can see the component list and the Apex test class list:

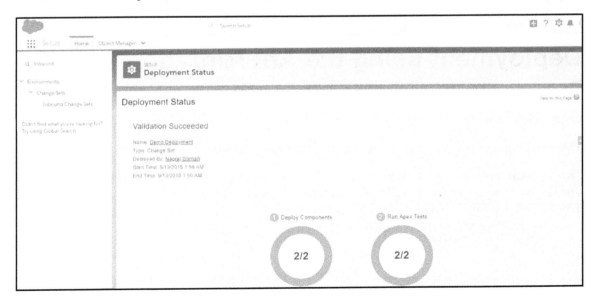

Now the Change Set is enabled for the quick deployment of validated Change Sets by skipping Apex tests as part of the deployment:

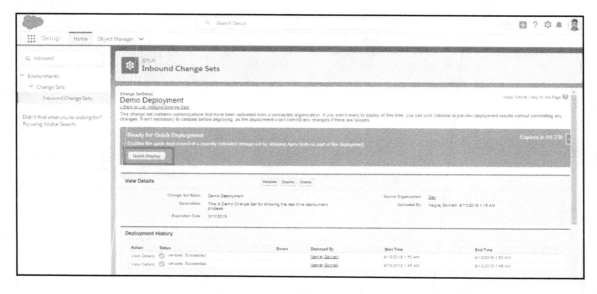

The Quick Deploy option

Now click on **Quick Deploy** to deploy the Change Set to the Production Organization.

Deployment using the Ant Migration Tool

The Ant Migration Tool provides a way to deploy metadata from the local directory to a Salesforce sandbox. We can use the Ant command-line utility to automate deployment tasks in Salesforce.

The Ant Migration Tool helps us to retrieve and deploy metadata to and from a sandbox.

This tool can also be used to take backups of your sandbox metadata. To configure access to the sandbox, we need to provide sandbox credentials in the `build.properties` file. The `build.xml` file contains commands for retrieving or deploying metadata. `Package.xml` contains the components to be retrieved or deployed.

The Ant Migration Tool is explained in detail via an example in `Chapter 4`, *Introduction to the Force.com Migration Tool.*

We will discuss some scenarios where the Ant Migration Tool deployment type can be used:

- Deployment can involve many setup changes, but using the web interface to make those changes is a difficult and time-consuming job. The Ant Migration Tool can be used to automate the process of making setup changes.
- Having multiple environments requires repeated deployment to the development, testing, and staging environments before any changes can be deployed to the production environment. Automating the retrieval and deployment of components will help to speed up that process.
- We can set up automated backups to occur at midnight, copying the metadata of the sandbox and restoring it whenever we need to.

Using the Force.com IDE to deploy Apex

The Force.com IDE is a plugin for the Eclipse IDE. The Force.com IDE provides a unified interface for building and deploying Salesforce applications. Designed for developers and development teams, the IDE provides tools for accelerating Salesforce application development, including source code editors, test execution tools, wizards, and integrated help. This tool includes basic color-coding, outline view, integrated unit testing, and auto-compilation on save with error-message display capability.

The Force.com IDE is a free resource provided by Salesforce to support its users and partners, but isn't considered part of our services in terms of the Salesforce Master Subscription Agreement.

To deploy Apex from a local project in the Force.com IDE to a Salesforce organization, use the Deploy to Server wizard.

If you're deploying to a Production Organization, at least 75% of your Apex code must be covered by unit tests, and all of those tests must complete successfully.

Note the following:

- When deploying components to the Production Organization, all test classes in the organization are executed by default
- There should be at least 1% test coverage in every trigger
- All components should be compiled successfully
- Test classes and test methods are not counted as part of Apex code coverage
- Some parts of the code are not counted in Apex code coverage; for example, debugs, comments, and spaces are not included

To use the Force.com IDE, we must first install Eclipse. Once Eclipse has been installed, follow these steps to install the Force.com IDE:

1. Open Eclipse:

2. Now enter the **Workspace** path and click **OK**:

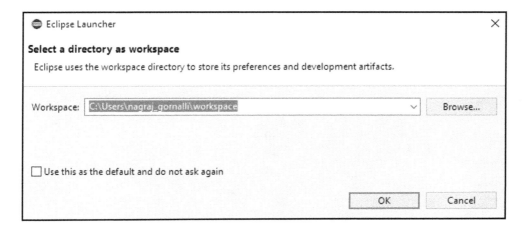

3. Now select **Help** and click on **Install New Software**:

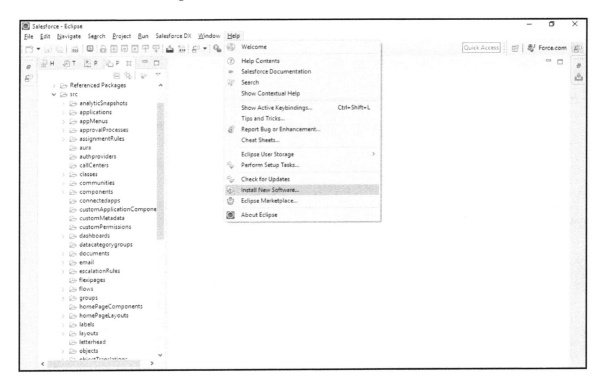

4. To add new software, hit the **Add...** button.

5. In the **Add Repository** dialog box, enter the name as `Force.com` and enter the location as `https://developer.salesforce.com/media/force-ide/eclipse45`:

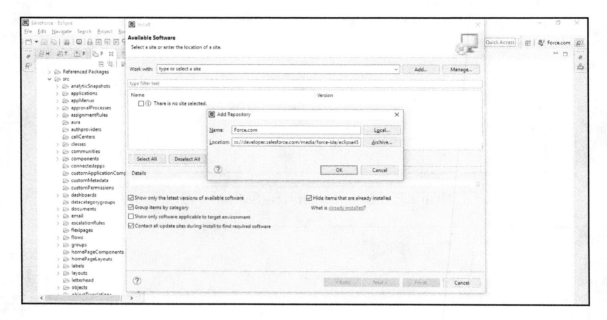

We will get a list of everything related to the Force.com IDE:

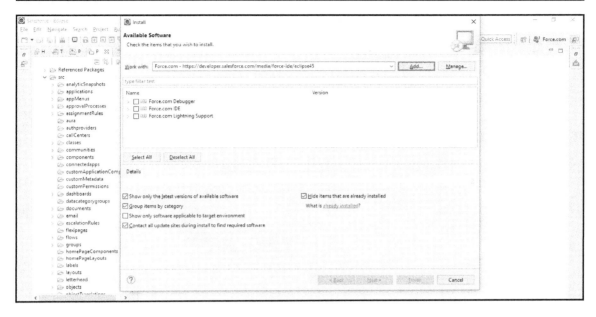

List of available software

6. We need to select the **Force.com IDE**. We can add additional software, such as **Force.com Debugger** and **Force.com Lightning Support**:

7. Click on **Next** to proceed. If there are any issues, we can cancel the installation:

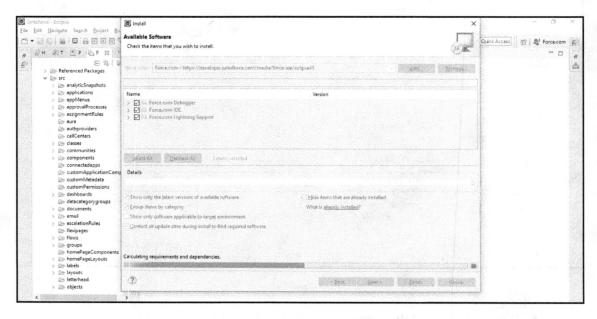

Installing the required software

8. Select the **Keep my installation the same and modify the items being installed to be compatible** radio button. To proceed, click on **Next**. Again, if there are any issues, we can cancel the installation:

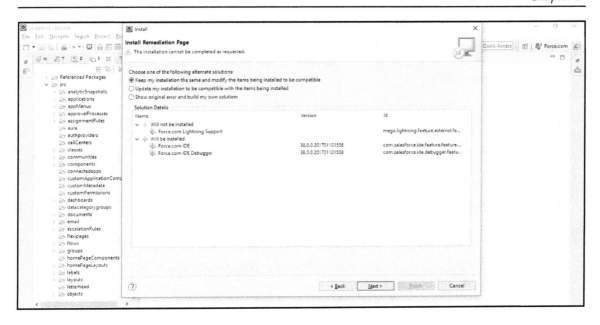

9. In **Review Licenses**, accept the terms and click **Finish**:

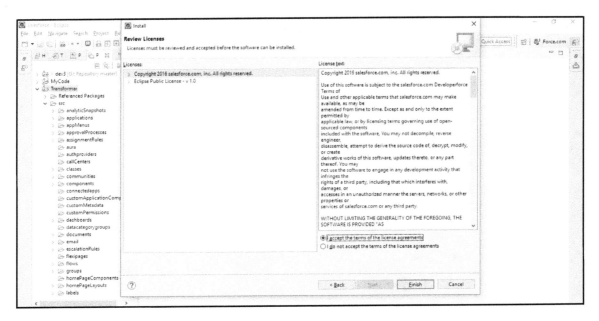

10. Click **OK** to proceed. Now Eclipse successfully installs the Force.com IDE and the required dependencies. When the installation is complete, you will be prompted to restart. Click on **Restart Now**. Here only Eclipse will restart, not your machine:

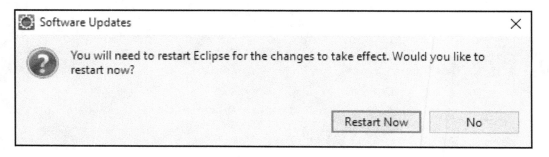

11. Wait for Eclipse to restart. Now select the **Window** tab and, in the **Open Perspective** tab, select **Other**.
12. Select **Force.com** and click **OK**.

Follow these steps to deploy code from Force IDE:

1. First, we need to open the project. Then right-click on **Project**, which will show many options. Select **Force.com** and click on **Project Properties**:

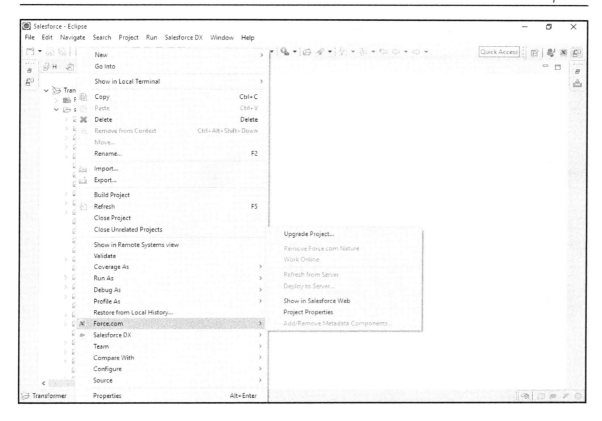

Here we need to create a connection to the organization by using the credentials. Fill in all the details; that is, the **Username**, **Password**, and **Security Token**.

2. Select the **Environment** as **Production/Developer Edition**:

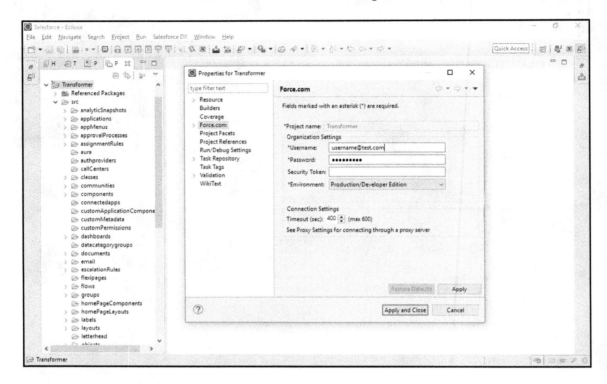

3. Hit the **Apply and Close** button:

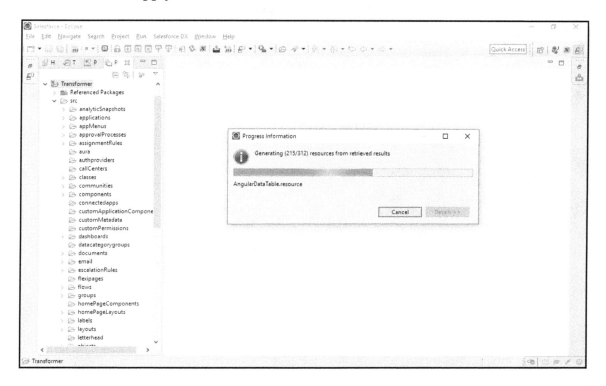

4. Once again, right-click on **Project**. We will see many options there; select **Force.com** and click on **Deploy to Server...**:

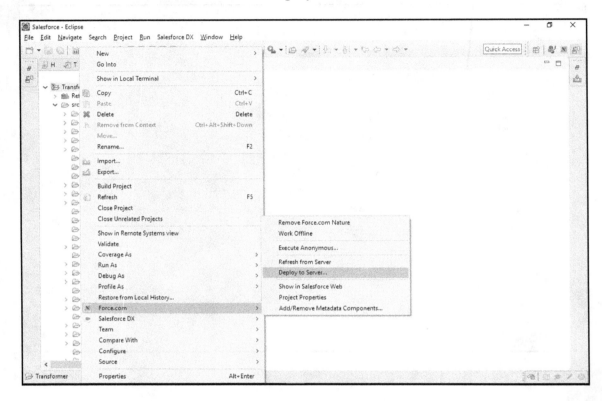

Here we need to add the credentials. Fill in all the details (in the **Username**, **Password**, and **Security Token** fields):

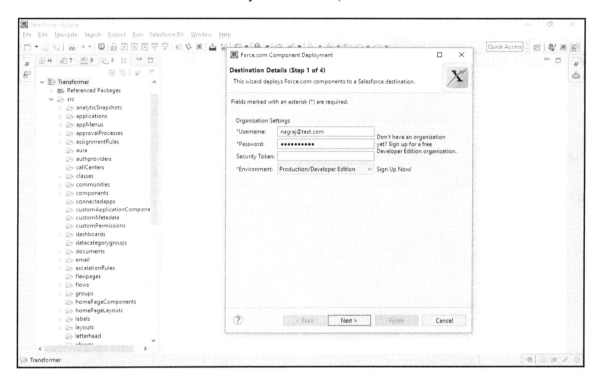

5. Hit the **Next** button. A window will appear showing a list of metadata components:

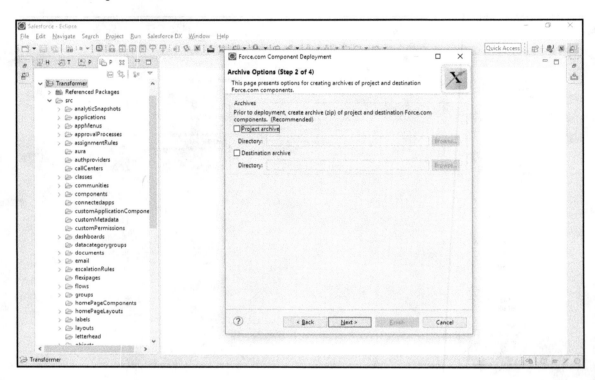

6. Select the components to be deployed via the relevant checkboxes:

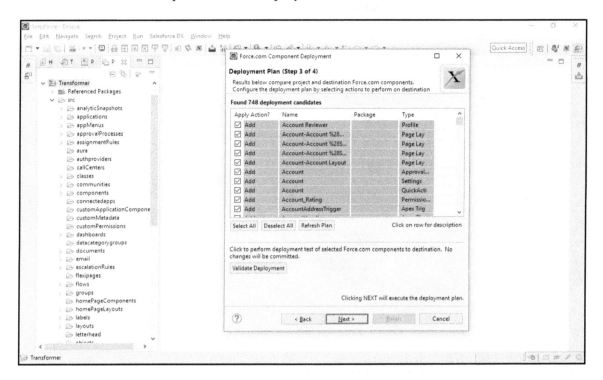

7. To validate the components, click **Validate Deployment**. We must validate all components before actual deployment takes place:

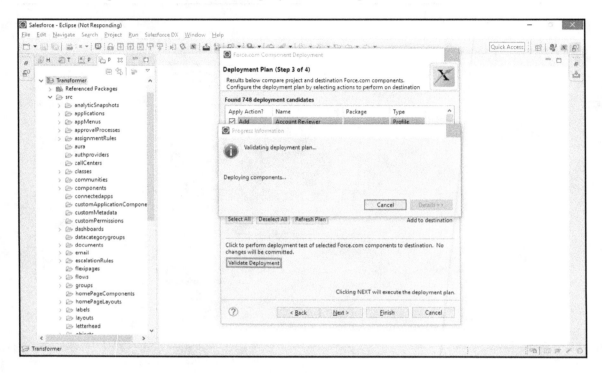

8. Once the validation is successfully done, click **Next**. All of the selected components will be deployed to the Salesforce organization.

Installing Salesforce DX plugins to Visual Studio Code

Perform the following steps to set up Visual Studio Code:

1. Download and install the latest version of Visual Studio Code from `https:// code.visualstudio.com/download`.

2. After installation, open Visual Studio Code and, on the left toolbar, click the **Extensions** icon. Search for **Salesforce Extensions for VS Code**:

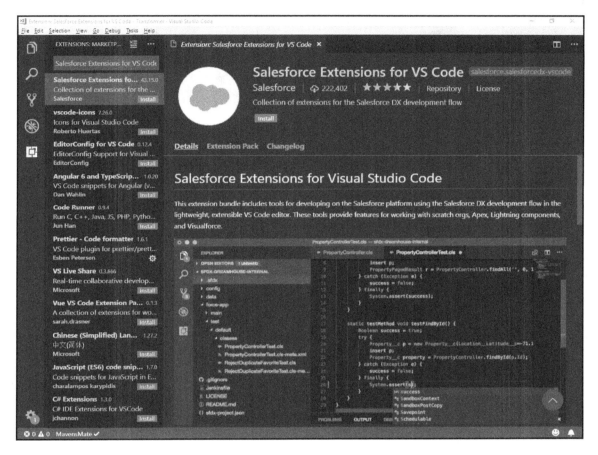

Search results for Salesforce Extensions for VS Code

3. Click on the relevant **Install** button to install the extension pack:

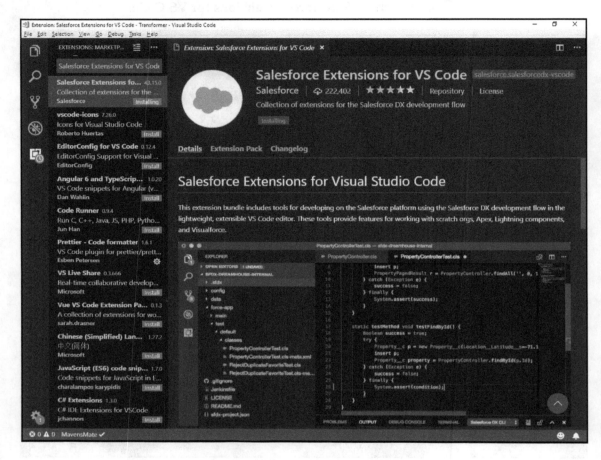

Installing the required extension

4. Once the installation is complete, click on the **Reload** button:

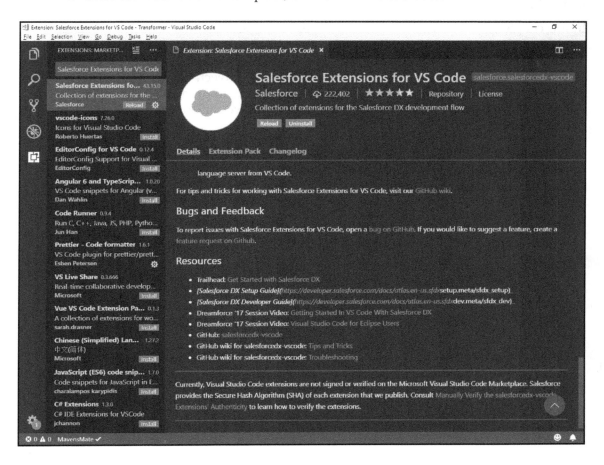

Summary

In this chapter, we learned about how to deploy Salesforce code from one sandbox to other sandbox, from the sandbox to a Production Organization, and from one organization to another organization. We were introduced to the different types of code deployment. We also learned how to use them depending on the type of project. We learned about how we can use Change Sets and the Force.com IDE to move code to production when we are working on projects where we need to continuously move code to production, such as in an ongoing project.

In the agile methodology, we mostly use the Ant Migration Tool, enabling code to be moved at specific intervals or in sprints. In the next chapter, we will discuss the Ant Migration Tool in greater depth.

Introduction to the Force.com Migration Tool

4

In the previous chapter, we saw how Salesforce deployment is done in traditional ways. We learned about change set deployment, inbound and outbound changes in Salesforce, how to use Eclipse to deploy code to a sandbox, and Ant scripts as well. Also, we compared deployment methods in Salesforce with their advantages and disadvantages and learned how to choose the appropriate method of deployment according to our use case.

In this chapter, we will study the Force.com Migration Tool in detail. We will discover how to install and set up the Force.com Migration Tool. Also, we will see how to use the migration tool to retrieve metadata components from a Salesforce sandbox and deploy them in another sandbox. Also, we will explain some important operations such as deploy code and undeploy code. We will discuss about configuration files involved in sandbox operations.

We are going to explain the complete process for retrieving metadata from a sandbox and constructing a project manifest. We will learn how to configure sandbox credentials in Force.com Migration Tool to perform operations like deploy or delete metadata files from a sandbox.

In this chapter, we will learn about the following topics:

- What the Force.com Migration Tool is?
- How to set up the Force.com Migration Tool
- How the Force.com tool helps developers and DevOps
- Using the migration tool to retrieve metadata from a sandbox
- Deploying metadata on a sandbox
- Deleting files/components from a Salesforce organization using `destructiveChanges.xml`
- Troubleshooting

What the Force.com Migration Tool is?

The Force.com Migration Tool provides a scripted way to deploy or retrieve metadata to and from a Salesforce sandbox. It is based on Ant/Java.

The Force.com Migration Tool helps us to copy Salesforce components from one organization easily. In normal practice, we have different environments such as development, test, UAT, and production. As developers develop components in a Developer sandbox, they need to move those changes to test or UAT for testers to test and give the green light for a feature/change to production. However, this is not a one-time process. Often, features or changes do not work properly or they introduce some bugs, testers raise an issue/bug, and developers start working on them. Once the bug/issue is fixed in the development environment, we need deployment of the change to test/UAT again. So, this is a repetitive process due to many reasons. Doing this deployment using a change set every time is not a convenient option, hence we need a solution to perform this task that is fast, easy, and less error-prone.

The Ant Migration Tool provides a solution to all of the problems we just discussed. The Ant Migration Tool is easy to set up and use. Once setup is done, only a few more things need to be changed for repetitive use. Ant migration tasks can be scripted, so we can easily automate most of your daily tasks. The Force.com Migration Tool is a Salesforce-supported tool; we don't have to worry much about its compatibility with your application and security.

Setting up the Force.com Migration Tool

For setting up the Force.com Migration Tool, you need to install some prerequisites as mentioned in the following section. We can set up the migration tool on Windows, Mac, or Linux operating systems. The following are the steps for setting up the Force.com Migration Tool on a Linux machine.

Prerequisites

The prerequisites for setup are as follows:

- Java 1.7.x or later
- Ant tool

Let's install them on our system.

Java

Java version 1.7.x or later is recommended for better security. Check whether Java is already installed on your system using the command line as shown:

1. Open the Terminal.
2. Type `java -version` and press *Enter*.

You will see the following output:

```
java version "1.7.0_21"
Java(TM) SE Runtime Environment (build 1.7.0_21-b11)
Java HotSpot(TM) 64-Bit Server VM (build 23.21-b01, mixed mode)
```

If Java is not installed on the system, use the following instructions to install Java:

1. Visit `http://www.oracle.com/technetwork/java/javase/downloads/index.html`.
2. Download the latest version of the Java JDK. Install the JDK.
3. Verify by typing `java -version` at Command Prompt.

Ant

To check the Ant version installed, you need to perform the following steps:

1. Open the Terminal.
2. Run the `ant -version` command to verify whether Ant is installed on the system.

The output will be as follows:

```
ant -version
Apache Ant(TM) version 1.10.1 compiled on February 2 2017
```

If Ant is not installed on your system, then use following steps to install Ant:

The recommended Ant version is 1.5.x or later; you will need to download the latest version of Ant.

1. Download Apache Ant from `http://ant.apache.org/bindownload.cgi`. You need to download an Ant version above 1.6 in `ANT_HOME`. Note that, in our case, it is `/usr/local/`:

   ```
   $wget http://www-eu.apache.org/dist//ant/binaries/apache-ant-
   1.9.13-bin.tar.gz
   ```

2. Unzip Apache Ant to `ANT_HOME`:

   ```
   $unzip apache-ant-1.9.13-bin.tar.gz
   ```

3. Add the `bin` directory to your path .
4. Add the Ant binary path to the `.bashrc` file as shown:

   ```
   export JAVA_HOME=/usr/lib/jvm/java-1.8.0
   export PATH=$PATH:$JAVA_HOME/bin
   export ANT_HOME=/usr/local/apache-ant-1.9.13
   export PATH=$PATH:$ANT_HOME/bin
   ```

For more information, see `http://ant.apache.org/manual/install.html`.

Installing the Ant Migration Tool on Linux

The installation steps are as follows:

1. Download the Force.com Migration Tool from `https://developer.salesforce.com/page/Force.com_Migration_Tool`:

   ```
   #wget https://gs0.Salesforce.com/dwnld/
   SfdcAnt/Salesforce_ant_39.0.zip
   ```

2. Save the `.zip` file locally and extract the contents to the directory of your choice:

#unzip Salesforce_ant_39.0.zip

Note that, in our case, it is `/home/devops/Force_com_tool`.

3. After unzipping `Salesforce_ant_39.0.zip`, you will find `ant-Salesforce.jar`; this is required to run Ant tasks. Copy `Salesforce_ant_39.0.zip` to another folder named `Sample`, which has examples for deploying and retrieving metadata from a sandbox in `codepkgclasses`, `removecodepkg`. Also the `Sample` folder contains a `build.properties` file where we provide credentials to access Salesforce sandboxes. The `Build.xml` file has Ant tasks mentioned, which use credentials from `build.properties`.

Installing the Ant Migration Tool on Windows

To use the Ant Migration Tool on a Windows machine, we need Java and Ant installed on the machine. The steps to install Java and Ant are mentioned in the previous section.

The following steps are needed to set the `ANT_HOME` environment variable on Windows:

1. Enter `environment` in the search box:

2. Select **Edit the system environment variables**. Under the **Advanced** tab, select **Environment Variables**:

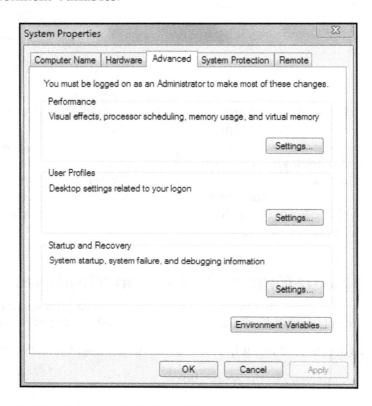

3. Under **System Environment Variables**, create a new ANT_HOME environment variable. Set the value of ANT_HOME to the Ant binary path:

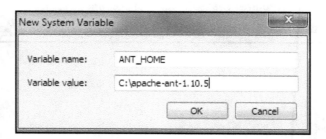

4. Create a new environment variable with the name ANT_OPTS and value – Xms256M:

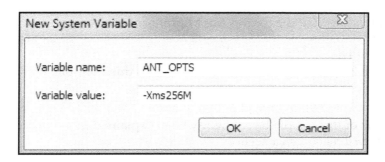

5. Edit the Path environment variable and add the ANT_HOME path as shown in the following screenshot. Click on **OK**. Again click on **OK** to save the environment variable:

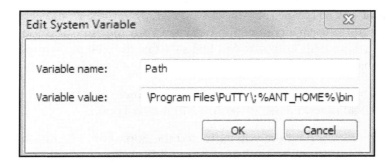

6. Open Command Prompt and check the Ant version using the ant – version command. You will see the output as follows:

```
Apache Ant(TM) version 1.10.5 compiled on July 10 2018
```

Installing the Salesforce Ant Migration Tool

The installation steps are as follows:

1. Download the ZIP file for the Ant Migration Tool from `https://developer.salesforce.com/docs/atlas.en-us.daas.meta/daas/forcemigrationtool_install.htm`
2. Save the ZIP file to any directory you like. In this example, we will be using a `Demo` folder at the `C:\Demo` path.
3. Extract `Salesforce_ant_43.0.zip` to `C:\Demo\Salesforce_ant_43.0`. The contents of the ZIP file have already been explained in the *Installing the Ant Migration Tool on Linux* section.

Retrieving metadata from a sandbox

To start retrieving metadata from a sandbox, we need to configure `build.xml`, `package.xml`, and `build.properties`. The `build.properties` file is used to specify Salesforce credentials to form a connection between your machine and the Salesforce sandbox. The `build.xml` file contains Ant tasks that need to be performed in the sandbox. package.xml is project manifest it will contain packages to retrieve or deploy.

We will go through the common procedure to retrieve metadata from a Salesforce organization to a local machine using the Ant Migration Tool:

1. Go to the location where you extracted the Force.com Migration Tool `.zip` file. You need to edit the `build.properties` file using any editor.
2. In this case, we will use vim editor. Run the following command:

   $vim build.properties

3. Let's have a look at the sample `build.properties` file:

```
build.properties
sf.username = devopsxxx@Salesforce.com.dev
sf.password = mypassxxxxxxxxxxxxxxxxxxxxxxxxx
sf.token = <Security Token Generated>
#sf.sessionId = <Insert your Salesforce session id here. Use this
or username/password above. Cannot use both>
#sf.pkgName = <Insert comma separated package names to be
retrieved>
#sf.zipFile = <Insert path of the zipfile to be retrieved>
#sf.metadataType = <Insert metadata type name for which
listMetadata or bulkRetrieve operations are to be performed>
```

```
# Use 'https://login.Salesforce.com' for production or developer
edition (the default if not specified).
# Use 'https://test.Salesforce.com for sandbox.
sf.serverurl = https://test.Salesforce.com <ForSandbox>
sf.maxPoll = 20
# If your network requires an HTTP proxy, see
http://ant.apache.org/manual/proxy.html for configuration.
Load properties from file
```

4. Add the required login credentials for the desired Salesforce organization, such as the following:

   - `Sf.username`: This field specifies the Salesforce username for your sandbox/production. The username provided should have permission to **Modify All Data**. If you are connecting to your sandbox instance, then you need to append your sandbox name to your username.

     For example, if you can specify username as per you wish but it is good practice to have meaningful names , it will help us to identify sandbox. If your username is `xxx@Salesforce.com` and you want to connect with sandbox `dev` then the `sf.username` value can be `xxx@Salesforce.com.dev`.

   - `Sf.password`: This field specifies the password for your Salesforce username. You need to append a Salesforce security token to the password. A security token is 25-digit case-sensitive code that is used for authenticating an API login. A security token is required when you are logging in using an API.

     For example, if your password is `mypass` and the security token is `xxxxxxxxxxxxxxxxxxxxxxxxx` then the value of the `sf.password` field should be `mypassxxxxxxxxxxxxxxxxxxxxxxxxx`.

If you don't have a security token, you can reset it. The steps to reset your security token are as follows:

1. Log in to your organization, and navigate to the top navigation bar. Go to <your name> | **My Settings** | **Personal** | **Reset My Security Token**:

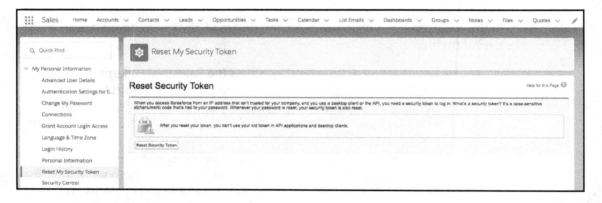

2. Click on **Reset Security Token**. This invalidates your existing token.
3. You will get your security token on your user's mail ID. For security reasons, the security token is not shown in the reset settings.

 Note: If you still face issues at login, you need to check whether you have set a **Login IP Range** such as 53.14.120.10 to 53.14.120.255. Then you need to delete the login IP range if you are not in the same IP range.

- `Sf.serverurl`: This field specifies the server URL for Salesforce. If you want to connect to a production organization or Developer Edition organization then the value of this field will be `https://login.Salesforce.com`. If you want to work with a sandbox then the value of field will be `https://test.Salesforce.com`.If you use custom domain then you can set value as `https://custom-domain.my.salesforce.com`.

5. Now we need to list out all components we want to retrieve from the sandbox. The `package.xml` file is a project manifest where we list all the components we want to retrieve or deploy. In our `package.xml` file, we have mentioned all Apex class components in the project. If you want to take a backup of your sandbox metadata, then you can mention all components in `package.xml`. For example, `package.xml` is for Apex classes only:

```
<?xml version="1.0" encoding="UTF-8"?>
<Package xmlns="http://soap.sforce.com/2006/04/metadata">
    <types>
    <members>*</members>
    <name>ApexClass</name>
    </types>
    <version>36.0</version>
</Package>
```

6. The next file we need to configure is `build.xml`. This file specifies a target to retrieve and deploy metadata. Ant tasks are mentioned in the `build.xml` file. The configuration steps are as follows:

   1. Go to the directory where `build.xml` is situated

   2. Run the `ant` command to verify whether you have installed Apache Ant properly

   3. The `build.xml` file loads the `build.properties` file to get access to the sandbox

   4. To retrieve metadata from your sandbox, user parameters can be set for each `<sf:retrieve>` target

   5. As our retrieve target is `DevOps/src`, all metadata will be stored in this directory

   For example, take a look at the following `build.xml` file:

```
<project name="Force.com Migration Tool"
default="retrieveUnpackaged" basedir="."
xmlns:sf="antlib:com.Salesforce">
<taskdef uri="antlib:com.Salesforce"
        resource="com/Salesforce/antlib.xml"
        classpath="lib/ant-Salesforce.jar"
    />
    <!-- Load properties from file -->
    <property file="build.properties"/>
    <!-- Load properites from environment -->
    <!-- These will override properties from the file -->
        <property environment="env"/>
        <property name="sf.username"
```

```
                              value="${env.SF_USERNAME}"/>
                    <property name="sf.password"
          value="${env.SF_PASSWORD}"/>
                    <property name="sf.token" value="${env.SF_TOKEN}"/>
                    <property name="sf.serverurl"
          value="${env.SF_SERVERURL}"/>

                    <!-- Retrieve an unpackaged set of metadata from your
          org -->
                    <!-- The attribute 'unpackaged' is where metadata will
          be stored -->
                    <target name="retrieveUnpackaged">
                    <!-- Retrieve the contents into another directory -->
                          <sf:retrieve
                                username="${sf.username}"
                                password="${sf.password}${sf.token}"
                                serverurl="${sf.serverurl}"
                                retrieveTarget="DevOps/src"
                                unpackaged="${basedir}/package.xml"
                          />
                    </target>
              <!-- Retrieve the information on all supported metadata
          types -->
          </project>
```

7. Retrieve metadata using the `ant` command. Run the following command to retrieve Apex class metadata in the retrieve target, that is, `DevOps/src`:

   $ ant -file build.xml

8. The console log is shown in the following screenshot:

```
11:36:42 [test1] $ /usr/local/apache-ant-1.10.1/bin/ant -file build.xml
11:37:09 Buildfile: /var/lib/jenkins/workspace/Retrive_SandBox_to_Git/test1/build.xml
11:37:11
11:37:11 retrieveUnpackaged:
11:37:31 [sf:retrieve] Request for a retrieve submitted successfully.
11:37:31 [sf:retrieve] Request ID for the current retrieve task: 09S6E0000005wgpUAA
11:37:31 [sf:retrieve] Waiting for server to finish processing the request...
11:37:31 [sf:retrieve] Request Status: InProgress
11:37:42 [sf:retrieve] Request Status: InProgress
11:37:52 [sf:retrieve] Request Status: InProgress
```

If the build is successful, then it will show a BUILD SUCCESSFUL message.

Deploying metadata on a sandbox

We saw in the previous example how we can retrieve metadata from a sandbox and deploy to a local environment. We can use Eclipse to edit and make changes in code or add new feature code. Developers can use the Force.com migration plugin to sync metadata with a workspace in Eclipse. After making changes in code, developers can deploy changes on a test/UAT sandbox. We can use the Force.com Migration Tool to deploy changes to the sandbox.

We will go through the common procedure to deploy metadata to a Salesforce organization from a local machine using the Ant Migration Tool. To provide access to the sandbox, we need to add sandbox credentials in the `build.properties` file as we provided credentials in *Step 3* in the *Retrieve metadata from sandbox* section previously. The value of the `Sf.serverurl` field will depend on where you want to deploy your changes. If you want to deploy on test, UAT sandbox, or any other development sandbox, then it will be `https://test.Salesforce.com`. If you are deploying your changes to the production environment, then use `https://login.Salesforce.com`. But until all test cases are successfully passed, we should not deploy any changes to the production environment directly; this can introduce failure in existing features and break the application.

Once we are done with changes in `build.properties`, we need to add all the components we want to deploy to the sandbox in `package.xml`:

```
<project name="Force.com Migration Tool" default="retrieveUnpackaged"
basedir="." xmlns:sf="antlib:com.Salesforce">
<taskdef uri="antlib:com.Salesforce"
        resource="com/Salesforce/antlib.xml"
        classpath="lib/ant-Salesforce.jar"
    />
        <property environment="env"/>
        <property name="sf.username" value="${env.SF_USERNAME}"/>
        <property name="sf.password" value="${env.SF_PASSWORD}"/>
        <property name="sf.token" value="${env.SF_TOKEN}"/>
        <property name="sf.serverurl" value="${env.SF_SERVERURL}"/>

            <sf:deploy
              username="${sf.username}"
              password="${sf.password}${sf.token}"
              serverurl="${sf.serverurl}"
              deployRoot="DevOps/src"
              maxPoll="1000"
                                testLevel="NoTestRun"
                                pollWaitMillis="10000"
                                rollbackOnError="true"
        />
```

```
        </target>
    </project>
```

In the preceding file, there are some new parameters, such as the following:

- `deployRoot`: This is a mandatory parameter. All files to deploy will be there in this directory.
- `maxPoll`: This is an optional parameter. This parameter defines the number of times to poll the server for the results of the deploy request. It has 200 as the default value.
- `testLevel`: This is an optional parameter that specifies which tests to run while deployment is done on a specific sandbox. The value of this parameter can be different depending on the type of sandbox and where deployment is going on. For a development sandbox, this is set to `NoTestRun` as default where no tests will run. You can specify other options where you can choose which test cases to run or run all tests on organization that we will see in more detail in `Chapter 7`, *Continuous Testing*.
- `pollWaitMillis`: This is an optional parameter that defines the number of milliseconds to wait while polling for results of the deployment. The default value of this parameter is 10,000, so we can set this accordingly.

Deleting files/components from a Salesforce organization using destructiveChanges.xml

We have seen we can retrieve metadata from a sandbox, and we can deploy changes to a sandbox using the Ant Migration Tool. But sometimes we don't need some features and we want to delete some components or files such as objects, fields, and so on from our Salesforce organization. We need to create one more file along with `package.xml` that is `destructiveChanges.xml`. The format of the `destructiveChanges.xml` delete manifest will be the same as `package.xml`, only wildcard characters are not accepted in a delete manifest.

Delete component is same process as deploying components with delete manifest file. We need to add a list of the components to delete in `destructiveChanges.xml`. A sample file to delete a custom object is as follows:

```
<?xml version="1.0" encoding="UTF-8"?>
    <Package xmlns="http://soap.sforce.com/2006/04/metadata">
    <types>
        <members>MyTestObject__c</members>
```

```
        <name>CustomObject</name>
    </types>
</Package>
```

To deploy destructive changes, we need `package.xml` that contains only an API version. It should not contain any list of components. The `destructiveChanges.xml` and `package.xml` files should be in same directory.

How the Force.com tool helps developers and DevOps

The Force.com Migration Tool provides developers with a way to easily perform operations on their sandbox, such as retrieving, deploying, and deleting metadata. Using the Force.com Migration Tool, developers can deploy code to different sandboxes and switch between workspaces on Eclipse. The Migration Tool is easy to set up on developers' machines, and it provides a secure way to communicate with your Salesforce organization.

We can face issues if something goes wrong with deployments; having automated daily backup is very important in such scenarios. The Force.com Migration Tool provides a command-line way to retrieve the code and configuration from a Salesforce sandbox, so DevOps or admins can automate the task of taking a backup for your Salesforce organization code and configuration. Also, we can make use of open source continuous integration tools such as Jenkins to automate the process to take a backup of a Salesforce organization and save it to Git. In `Chapter 6`, *Continuous Integration*, we will cover using Jenkins to automate the Salesforce organization backup process step by step.

Troubleshooting

In this section, we will have a look at troubleshooting scenarios:

- **Connection issues**: The most common issue we face during retrieval or deploying metadata is a connection issue. We use asynchronous types of requests during retrieval or deployment of metadata so we do not get a response immediately. The call for deploy operation is asynchronous sometimes Ant Migration Tool time outs during deployment. So if the Ant Migration Tool fails due to timeout and the deployment has any errors, we will not be able to see the error logs. In that case, we need to configure the `pollWaitMillis` and `maxPoll` parameters.

- **Invalid credentials or user locked out**: If you are getting this error, then there is an issue with your `build.properties` file. You need to verify the username, password, security token, and server URL are correct. Also, if you have several failed login attempts, then there is chance that your user is locked out. So, the number of failed attempts that are allowed depends on your organization's settings. Sometimes, verifying proxy settings will also help to resolve issues with credentials.

- **Failed test cases**: If you are deploying changes to production, then as per Salesforce standards you need 75% code to be covered by test cases, and all test cases should pass to deploy code to a production environment successfully.

Summary

In this chapter, we learned about the Force.com Migration Tool and how to set up the tool in your environment. We have seen the step-by-step process to retrieve metadata from a sandbox using Ant scripts, and we learned about configuring our sandbox credentials in `build.properties` to provide access to a sandbox environment, listing components to retrieve in the `package.xml` project manifest, and retrieving the contents into the directory mentioned in the `build.xml` file.

After successfully retrieving metadata from a sandbox to a local machine, we moved to the next step, which is deploying changes to a sandbox. We have seen sample deployment of metadata using the Ant Migration Tool to a developer sandbox or test sandbox. Sometimes, we might need to delete components or files from a sandbox. We have seen how we can delete components from a Salesforce organization using `destructiveChanges.xml`.

In the next chapter, we will see what source control versioning is. We will also learn the advantages of using Git, branching strategy in Git, and how to set up a Git repository for your Salesforce project. We will also go through the developer flow of using Git with a code editor such as Eclipse.

5
Version Control

In the previous chapter, we looked at the Force.com migration tool. We went through a step-by-step procedure for setting up Force.com or the Ant migration tool on a Windows and Linux machine, studied the files that are required to retrieve metadata from a sandbox, and how to provide credentials to access a sandbox. We looked at the procedure to deploy metadata on sandboxes and discussed how Force.com helps developers and DevOps in everyday life.

In this chapter, we will study the source code versioning system and its types. We will mainly focus on Git distributed version control, and operations performed on the Git repository, such as commit, push, merge, and so on. We will also go through the step-by-step procedure for setting up our own GitLab server, adding a repository, adding users, and creating a branch. We will discuss Git branching strategies and protecting branches. Finally, we will learn how to use Git with a Salesforce project and how to save Salesforce metadata to Git.

What is meant by SCVS?

Source Code Versioning System (**SCVS**) as the name indicates, it helps to manage source code changes over time. There are many source control versioning systems available such as CVS, SVN, Git, and so on. Version control maintains the history of every file change, and helps developers to track changes in an application. The main reasons behind having a version control system are to be able track changes in an application and to be able to revert back if something goes wrong. As code undergoes various changes, version control helps us to maintain a working version of code, and with the help of versioning, we can also maintain different environments such as testing, staging, and production. Multiple users can work on the same application source code simultaneously using version control.

There are two varieties of version control, centralized and distributed. In centralized version control, there is one central repository where each user gets their own working copy. If anyone commits their changes to the source control system, other co-users can get those changes by updating their working copy. Subversion and CVS are centralized version systems.

In distributed version control, each user gets a local repository and working copy. Changes made by the user are saved in their local repository when they commit code. Co-users can get those changes when the user pushes the changes to the remote repository.

Version control in Salesforce

Salesforce has a limited audit capability to track changes in a sandbox. Making changes in the production environment is risky, and we are not able to see versions of files or track changes in a sandbox.

Reverting code in Salesforce is a very difficult task if we don't have version control in place.

Why doesn't Salesforce provide its own version control? Salesforce was basically designed for users to get their application running on the cloud without much understanding of the code. We can build small applications in Salesforce with just clicks, so Salesforce didn't focus on having version control. In Salesforce, we can modify the Salesforce organization in place so we don't need to have code on a local machine.

Mostly people working on Salesforce think that there is lot of work involved in setting up version control for Salesforce, which is only required if we have large teams. To set up version control for Salesforce projects, developers and administrators need to learn how to use version control systems, and they might need some knowledge of the command-line instructions involved. But we have many integrations of Git where we don't need to know about commands as we can use buttons or tabs instead.

As we have mentioned here, Salesforce does not provide any in-built version control, so we need to set up a source code version control system. There are many version control systems, but the most popular version control system is Git. In the following section, we will go through the GitLab setup and using Git in a Salesforce project.

Introduction to Git

Git is a commonly used version control system invented by Linus Torvalds. It is a distributed type of version control which enables more than one developer to work on the same project simultaneously.

It helps to maintain versions of source code so that if anything goes wrong, you can always revert back to the working version of your source code. To use Git, you will need a repository that will store your source code and make it available to all who are working on it.

Git uses the GitHub as a hosting service for Git repositories, and so first of all, you will need a GitHub account so that you will be able to create a repository to store your source code. There are two types of repository:

- **Public repository:** You can host public repositories on GitHub for free. These repositories will be accessible to all, so if you are going to save your important source code on GitHub, you should not save it on a public repository.
- **Private repository:** These repositories are protected; nobody can access them unless you give them access. You have to pay for private repositories.

We have introduced GitHub, but for now we will be using GitLab. GitLab is a fully featured open source Git server that you can install on your server. GitLab is a database-backend web application and is available in both community and enterprise editions.

Let's move to our next point, which is setting up our own GitLab server.

Setting up a GitLab server on a Linux instance

To set up the server, an omnibus package installation is recommended. We will install the GitLab Community Edition on an Ubuntu 16.04 server. You can install GitLab on other operating systems such as Ubuntu, Centos, Debian, and so on; you can find a list here: `https://about.gitlab.com/installation/`. An omnibus package installation is the recommended method by GitLab itself, as the set up is easy and the upgrade process is also painless.

Prerequisites

GitLab recommends using a server with the following configuration:

- 2 cores
- 4 GB of RAM

Install the required packages before installing GitLab Community Edition:

```
$sudo apt-get update
$sudo apt-get install ca-certificates curl openssh-server postfix
```

For the Postfix installation, choose **Internet Site** when prompted. On the next screen, enter your server's domain name or IP address to configure the system that will send mail:

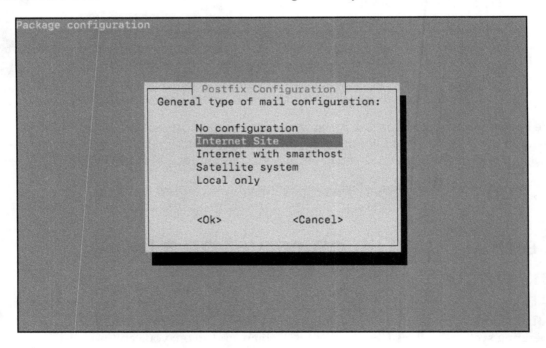

Let's move on to the GitLab server installation.

Installing the GitLab server

We have installed all required dependencies for the GitLab server. Run the following commands to install GitLab:

```
$curl -LO https://packages.gitlab.com/install/repositories
/gitlab/gitlab-ce/script.deb.sh
% Total    % Received % Xferd  Average Speed   Time    Time     Time
Current Dload  Upload   Total   Spent    Left  Speed
100  5933    0  5933    0      0  23796      0 --:--:-- --:--:-- --:--:--
23827
```

You can examine `script.deb.sh` and check all the packages that will be installed and their configuration, as you need to know what is being installed on your server. Once you have verified `script.deb.sh`, you are good to go for the next step in the installation:

```
$ sudo bash script.deb.sh
Detected operating system as Ubuntu/xenial.
Checking for curl...
Detected curl...
Checking for gpg...
Detected gpg...
Running apt-get update... done.
Installing apt-transport-https... done.
Installing /etc/apt/sources.list.d/gitlab_gitlab-ce.list...done.
Importing packagecloud gpg key... done.
Running apt-get update... done.
```

The repository is set up! You can now install packages.

This script will set up our server to use the GitLab maintained repositories. After completing this script, we will install the actual GitLab application with `apt`:

```
$sudo apt-get install gitlab-ce
```

This will install the required components on our system, and the GitLab configuration file is `/etc/gitlab/gitlab.rb`. You can edit the configuration file and reconfigure the GitLab server:

```
$sudo gitlab-ctl reconfigure
```

After installation is complete, visit your GitLab external URL and set up a password for the root user:

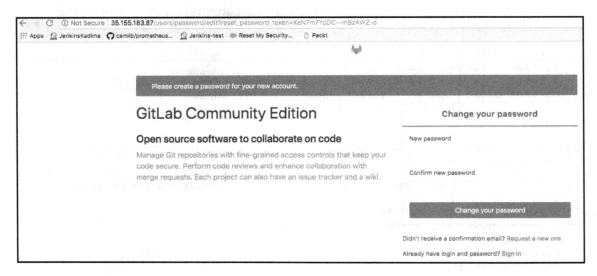

Log in with root user, and you will get the **Welcome** page for GitLab, as shown in this screenshot:

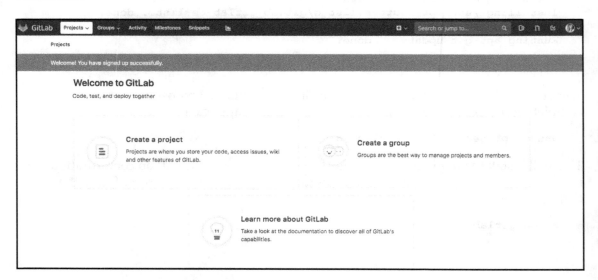

Now you have successfully set up GitLab, let's use it and create your first repository.

Creating your first project in GitLab

Log in to your GitLab server and follow the steps to create your first project repository:

1. Choose **Create a Project** to create a project on the GitLab server. In the project, we will store all our code, configuration, and other information related to our application.
2. Provide a project name and description. For now, we will create a sample Hello World node application. Our project name is `Sample`.
3. Next, comes the visibility level of your project; it can be public, internal, or private.
4. Public repositories can be cloned by anyone; any logged-in user can clone internal project repositories. To clone a private project, a user needs explicit access to clone the repository.
5. For now we will keep it public and check **Initialize repository with a README** for a quick start.
6. Click on **Create Project**:

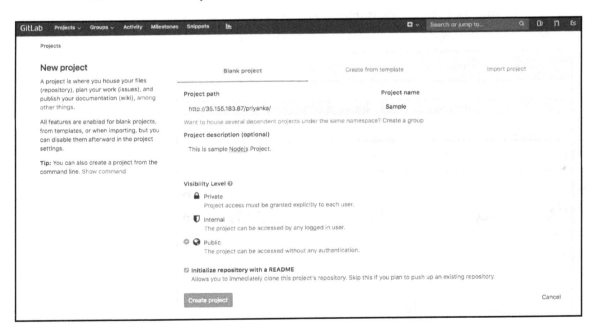

7. Clone the project URL:

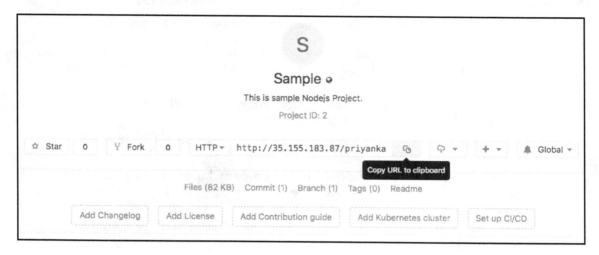

8. If you have Git commands installed on your machine, run the following command to clone the repository to your local machine:

```
$git clone http://35.155.183.87/root/Sample.git
Cloning into 'Sample'...
remote: Enumerating objects: 3, done.
remote: Counting objects: 100% (3/3), done.
remote: Total 3 (delta 0), reused 0 (delta 0)
Unpacking objects: 100% (3/3), done.
```

You will see the Readme.md file is already created in the Sample project. You are all set to start working with your Git repository:

Working with a Git repository

We have cloned the **Sample** repository on our local machine. Now we will see how to work with the Git repository:

1. Create a Node.js Hello World application that will create an HTTP server and respond to all requests on port 8080 with the string Hello World. Here is the sample code for the Node.js application:

```
var http = require("http");

http.createServer(function (request, response) {
```

```
// Send the HTTP header
// HTTP Status 200 OK
// Content Type is text/plain
response.writeHead(200, {'Content-Type': 'text/plain'});
// Send response body as "Hello World"
response.end('Hello World\n');
}).listen(8080);

// Print message
console.log('Server running at http://127.0.0.1:8080/');
```

2. Save the code in **main.js** and add this file to our Git repository.

3. Check untracked changes in our Git repository with following command:

```
$git status
On branch master
Your branch is up to date with 'origin/master'.
Untracked files:
  (use "git add <file>..." to include in what will be
committed)
    main.js
nothing added to commit but untracked files present (use "git
add" to track)
```

By default, GitLab sets **master** branch as our default branch. The newly added main.js file is not present on the remote repository, and it is also not tracked in the local Git.

Every file in the Git working directory is **tracked**, **untracked**, or **ignored**. The files which are committed or staged before are tracked files. Files that are not staged or committed are untracked files. The files that you don't want to add in the repository, such as files with credentials or machine-generated files, are mentioned in the .gitignore file.

An example of a .gitignore file coded to ignore all files with a .log extension is as follows:

```
.gitignore
# ignore all logs
*.log
```

4. Let's add the `main.js` file to the local repository; it needs to be indexed first. The `git add` command updates the index using the content found in the working directory. These changes will be staged for commit. You can add all changes into the index using `*` or the `-a` option in the `git add` command:

```
$git add .
$ git status
On branch master
Your branch is up to date with 'origin/master'.
Changes to be committed:
  (use "git reset HEAD <file>..." to unstage)
        new file:   main.js
```

5. The next step is to commit staged changes to the local repository:

```
$git commit -m "Add main.js file"
[master 9d8892d] Add main.js file
 1 file changed, 15 insertions(+)
 create mode 100644 main.js
```

The `commit` command is used to commit changes in the local repository. Other developers will not be able to see the changes. The important thing while committing your changes is to provide a commit message with the `-m` option in the command. Make sure your commit message relates to changes you're making in the code so that others using it will be able to understand your changes.

If you don't mention the filename, it will commit all the recent changes you made in the code.

The final step is to push your local changes to the remote repository; the push operation refers to pushing changes to the remote repository. While pushing changes, it is important to mention the origin of the changes:

```
$ git push origin master
Username for 'http://35.155.183.87': priyanka
Password for 'http://priyanka@35.155.183.87':
Counting objects: 3, done.
Delta compression using up to 4 threads.
Compressing objects: 100% (3/3), done.
Writing objects: 100% (3/3), 547 bytes | 547.00 KiB/s, done.
Total 3 (delta 0), reused 0 (delta 0)
To http://35.155.183.87/priyanka/Sample.git
   aad9bc9..9d8892d  master -> master
```

Git will ask you for your credentials to authenticate the user and the push changes to the remote repository hosted on the GitLab server. Now you will be able to see those changes in the GitLab web URL.

It will look like this:

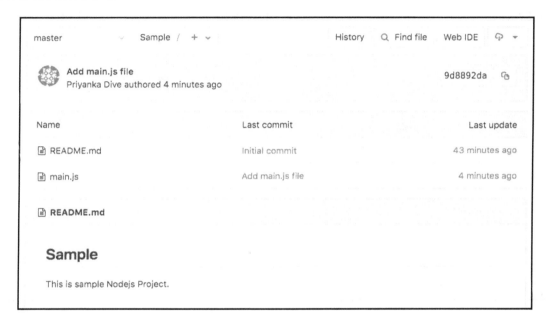

Viewing the commit history

You can check logs using the command line, switch to the Git repository and run the `git log` command, as shown here, to check the most recent commits. This command without any extra argument shows commits made in the repository in reverse order. The command output also contains information such as the SHA-1 checksum, the commit message, the date and time of the commit, and author details:

```
$git log
commit 9d8892da192fffb93a9a8a58fdf700632dabee3c (HEAD -> master,
origin/master, origin/HEAD)
Author: Priyanka Dive <user@example.com>
Date:   Mon Aug 27 00:56:39 2018 +0530

    Add main.js file
```

```
commit aad9bc971f4e69242e550f9e1771e23c1785b5e2
Author: priyanka <user@example.com>
Date:    Sun Aug 26 18:47:08 2018 +0000

        Initial commit
```

You can check Git commit messages with the timestamp and user details, as shown here:

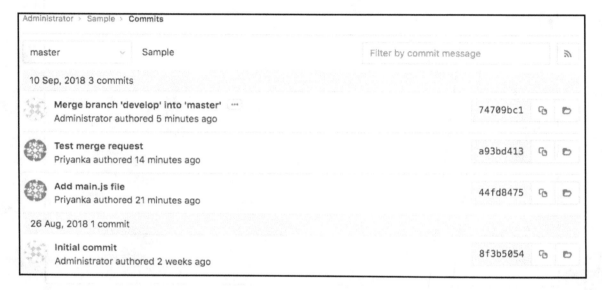

Adding a user to GitLab

The steps to add a user are as follows:

1. Log in to GitLab with admin user (root).
2. Click the spanner icon (top right) to enter **Admin area**:

3. You will see three buttons, **New project**, **New user**, and **New group**. Click on **New user**:

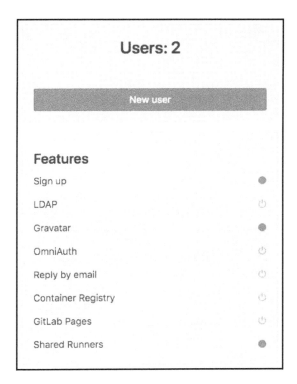

4. Fill in the required information – **Name**, **Username**, and **Email**:

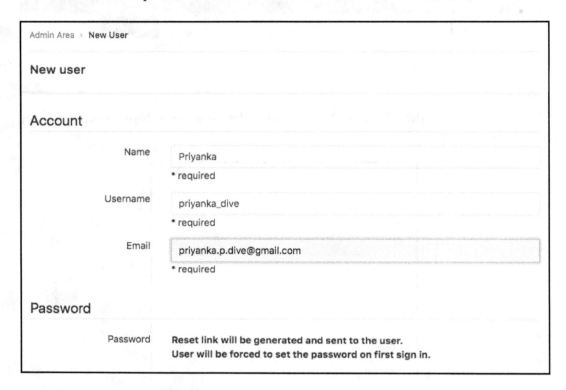

5. Provide a project user limit as per your organization's rules. Also, if you want a user to be able to create a group, give them access to creating a group by checking **Can create group**. If you want a user to have limited access, then select the **Access level** to be **Regular,** and if a user needs Admin privileges, then select the **Access level** to be **Admin** for the user:

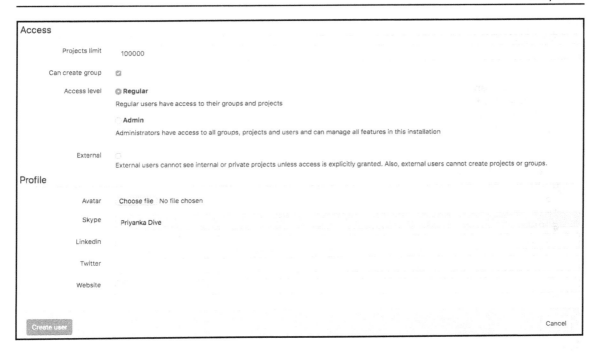

6. After filling in all the required information, click on **Create user**. This will create the user and send a password reset link to the user's Email ID.

Troubleshooting

Consider the following error:

```
There was an error running gitlab-ctl reconfigure:
execute[/opt/gitlab/embedded/bin/initdb -D /var/opt/gitlab/postgresql/data
-E UTF8] (postgresql::enable line 80) had an error:
Mixlib::ShellOut::ShellCommandFailed: Expected process to exit with [0],
but received '1'
---- Begin output of /opt/gitlab/embedded/bin/initdb -D
/var/opt/gitlab/postgresql/data -E UTF8 ----
STDOUT: The files belonging to this database system will be owned by user
"gitlab-psql".
This user must also own the server process.
STDERR: initdb: invalid locale settings; check LANG and LC_* environment
variables
---- End output of /opt/gitlab/embedded/bin/initdb -D
/var/opt/gitlab/postgresql/data -E UTF8 ----
Ran /opt/gitlab/embedded/bin/initdb -D /var/opt/gitlab/postgresql/data -E
UTF8 returned 1
```

Solution

This issue can be due to the LANG and LC_* variables, which are unset in the Linux system. In the omnibus installation, we can set these variables using the following commands and run the installation command again or reconfigure GitLab:

```
$export LC_ALL="en_US.UTF-8"
$export LC_CTYPE="en_US.UTF-8"
```

Branching strategy

Branching is a very useful feature provided by Git. It helps to develop multiple features in parallel. Branching can be useful to define environment specific codes such as develop, test, stage, and production. Usually, the environment to Git branch mapping will be, for example, the code for the development environment stored in the **develop** Git branch; for the test environment, we use the **test** Git branch, and so on. For the production environment, we use the **master** branch, as it is the first default branch created when we create any Git repository.

Let's see how we can create a branch using the web UI:

1. Log in to GitLab.
2. Go to your repository, **Sample**, that we created in the *Creating your first project in GitLab* section:

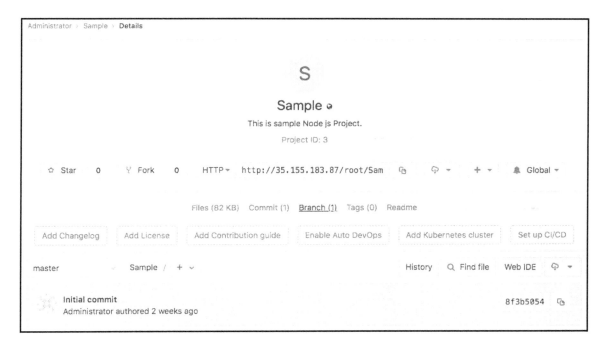

As you see in this screenshot, we have only one branch which is the master, and is the default branch.

3. Click on **Branch**, you will be redirected to a page where you can see all the active branches for this repository. Currently, we have a **master** branch:

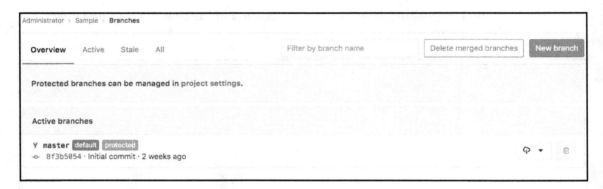

4. Click on **New branch**, type in the branch name, `develop`. We will be using this branch for development:

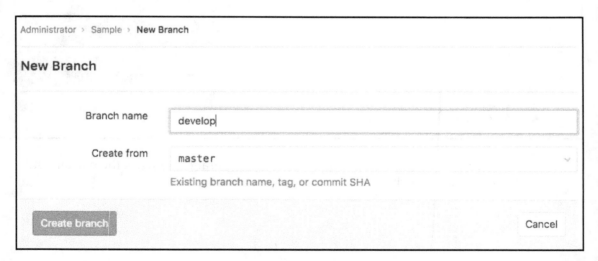

5. Click on **Create branch**. That's it. You can see the new branch that's been created from the master branch. You can now create another branch from the develop or master branch. As the develop branch is created from the master branch, all the code in the develop branch will be the same as in the master branch, for now:

6. Now, if we go to **Active Branches,** we can see two branches in the list. There is a difference between those two branches. The master branch is the default branch and the **protected** branch, but the newly created develop branch is not a protected branch. The only users who are authorized to make modifications in a protected branch are mostly senior developers or project leads. Due to this, we can avoid the problem of multiple developers simultaneously working on different features.

Handling branches using the Git CLI

After the Git clone, you will, by default, get code for the default branch set on your repository. In our case, it is the master branch. Let's check which branch we have cloned using the following command:

```
$git branch
* master
```

The asterisk in front of the branch name indicates a current branch.

Let's create a **test** branch:

```
$git branch test
```

This will create a new branch named test, on your local Git repository:

```
$git branch
* master
  test
```

Now you will see two branches in your local Git repository, the git branch <BRANCH_NAME> command will create a branch from the current branch. So, the **test** branch is created from the **master** branch.

Switch to the newly created the test branch and push it to the remote repository:

```
$git checkout test
Switched to branch 'test'
$git push origin test
Username for 'http://54.202.196.64': root
Password for 'http://root@54.202.196.64':
Total 0 (delta 0), reused 0 (delta 0)
remote:
remote: To create a merge request for test, visit:
remote:
http://54.202.196.64/root/Sample/merge_requests/new?merge_request%5Bsource_
branch%5D=test
remote:
To http://54.202.196.64/root/Sample.git
 * [new branch]      test -> test
```

Verify if you can see the **test** branch in the GitLab web UI:

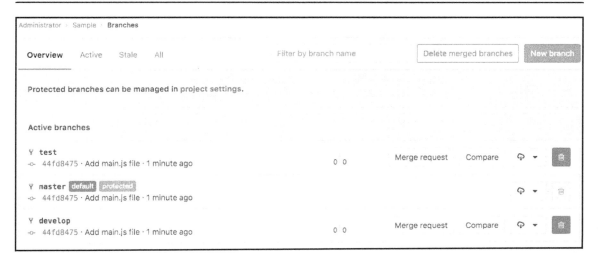

Merging changes from develop to master

Let's see how to merge changes from the develop branch to the master branch:

1. You can specify which branch to clone from the Git repository:

```
$git clone http://54.202.196.64/root/Sample.git -b develop
Cloning into 'Sample'...
remote: Enumerating objects: 6, done.
remote: Counting objects: 100% (6/6), done.
remote: Compressing objects: 100% (4/4), done.
remote: Total 6 (delta 0), reused 0 (delta 0)
Unpacking objects: 100% (6/6), done.
```

2. For testing, we will make a small change, such as changing the console log message from Hello World to Hello Git. Add the changes to Git and push the changes to the remote develop branch:

```
$git add main.js
$git commit -m "Test merge request"
$git push origin develop
Counting objects: 3, done.
Delta compression using up to 4 threads.
Compressing objects: 100% (3/3), done.
Writing objects: 100% (3/3), 321 bytes | 321.00 KiB/s, done.
Total 3 (delta 1), reused 0 (delta 0)
remote:
remote: To create a merge request for develop, visit:
```

```
remote:
http://54.202.196.64/root/Sample/merge_requests/new?merge_reque
st%5Bsource_branch%5D=develop
remote:
To http://54.202.196.64/root/Sample.git
44fd847..a93bd41  develop -> develop
```

3. If you want to create a merge request, open the URL shown in `remote`.

4. Assign it to the person who has the right to accept a merge request on the master branch:

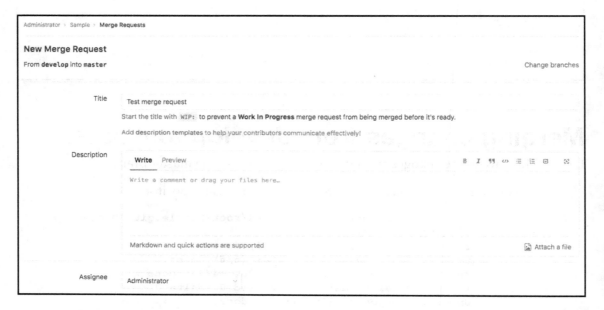

5. In our case, it is assigned to **Administrator**. Fill out the required information and click **Submit Merge Request**.

6. The Administrator user can see the merge request and, after verifying changes done by developers, if there are no merge conflicts and all previous checks are passed successfully, then the Administrator will accept the merge request by clicking on **Merge**. Changes in test will be moved to the master branch:

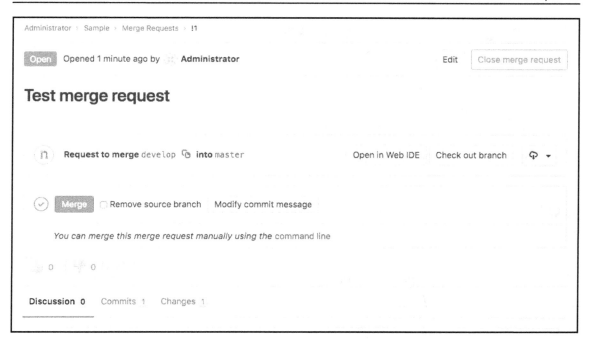

The Administrator can modify the commit message, and remove the source branch if it is not required afterwards. If something goes wrong, the Administrator can revert the changes as well:

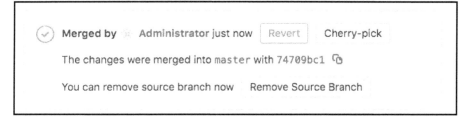

Using Git in the Eclipse IDE

Steps 1 to 3 are already explained in `Chapter 1`, *Salesforce Development and Delivery Process*:

1. Eclipse installation
2. Install the Force.com IDE plugin
3. Configure Force.com project in Eclipse

We will continue with the next steps in the following sections.

Configuring Git and pushing code to Git

Now we need to configure Git.

1. Create the repository in a new folder by right-clicking on the folder and selecting **Git repository here...**:

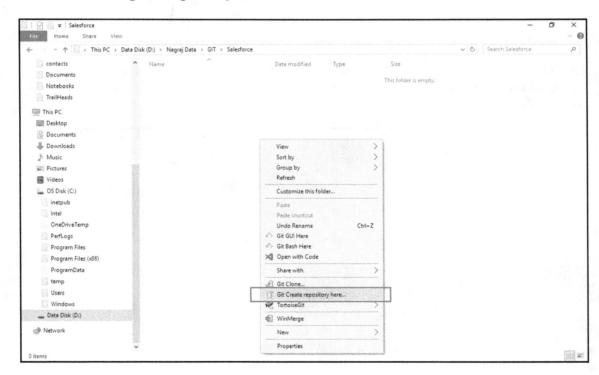

2. Here, we are not selecting the **Make it Bare** and click on **OK**:

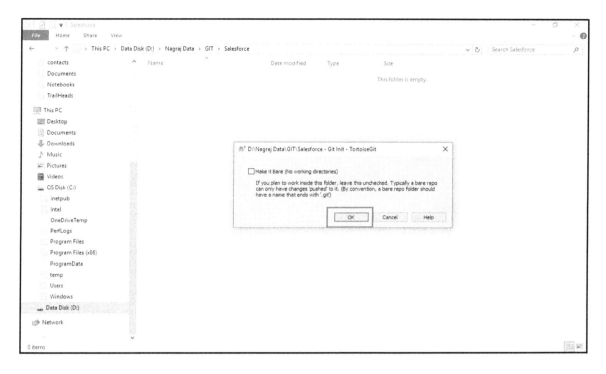

3. You will see the next screen. Click on **OK**:

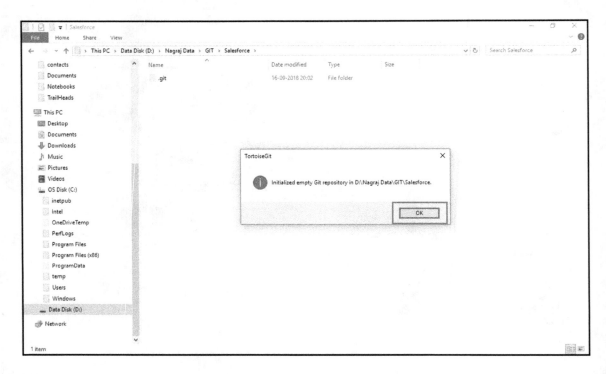

4. Right-click on the folder and select **TortoiseGit** and click on **Settings**:

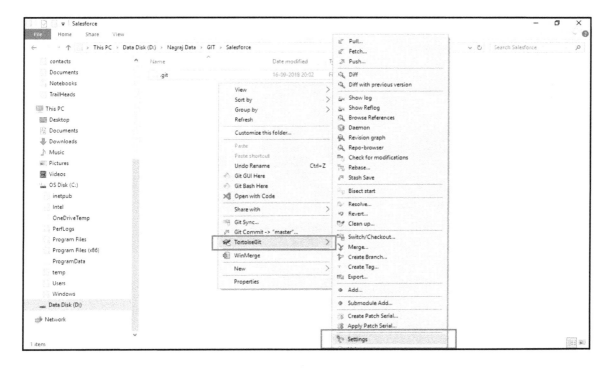

5. You will see the next screen. Click on **OK**:

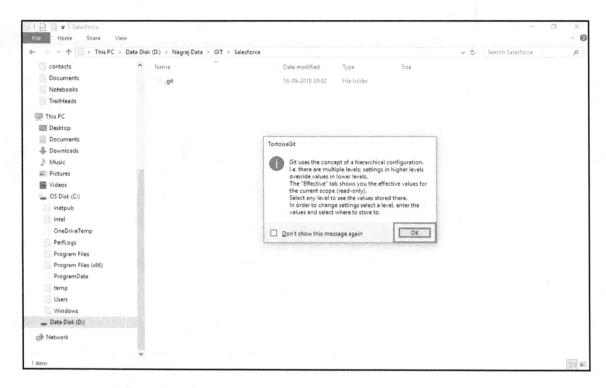

6. Select the Git and enter the **Name** and **Email**:

7. You will see the next screen. Select the Git and click on **Remote**:

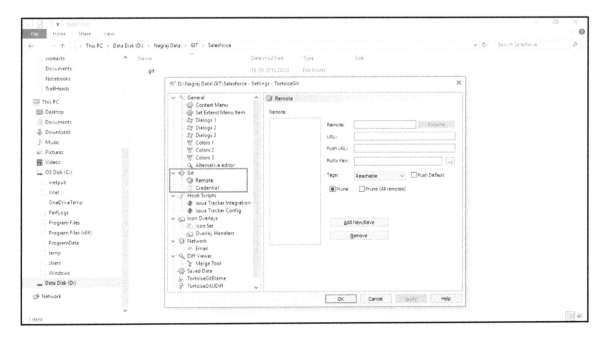

8. Open the Git project in the browser and select the project.

9. Copy the HTTP URL from the project:

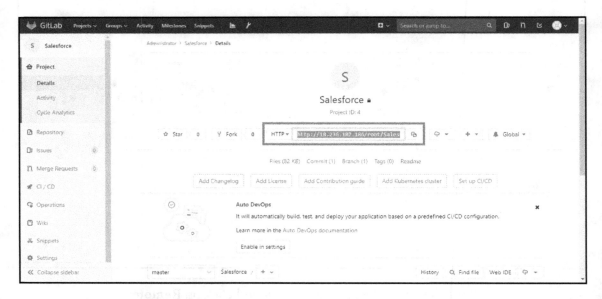

10. Enter the copied URL in **URL** and **Push URL**. Select **All** in the **Tags** field and click on the **Add New/Save** button:

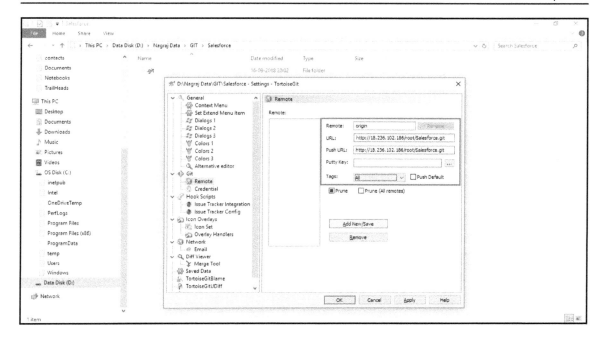

11. Click on the **Yes** button:

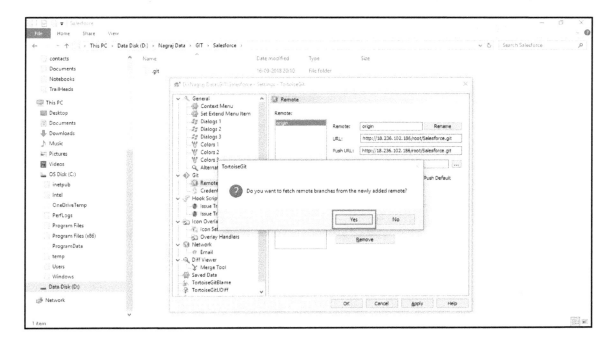

12. You will see this screen. Click on **OK**:

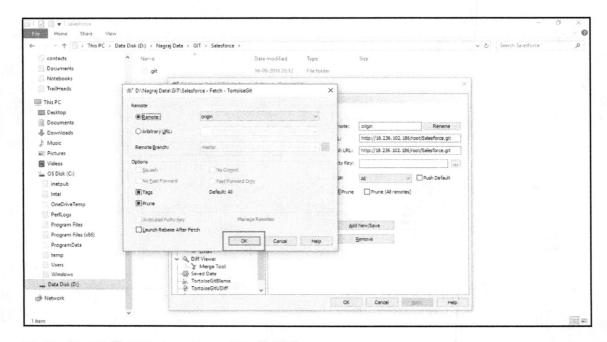

13. Enter the Git credentials in this screen:

14. Click on **OK**:

15. Once you have completed the process, click on the **Close** button:

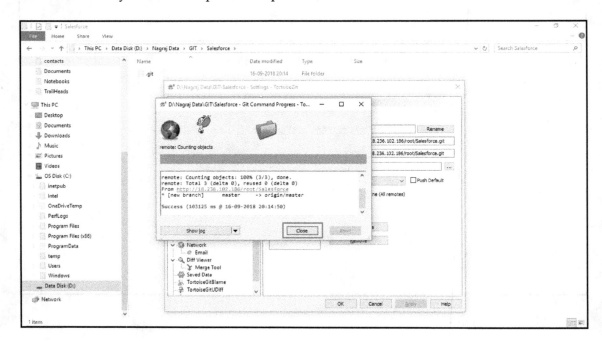

16. Finally, click on **OK**:

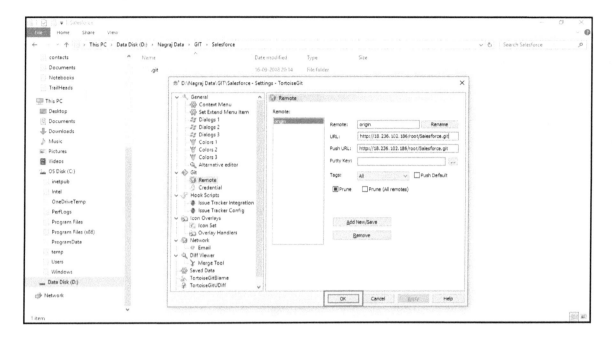

Now you have to pull the files from the Git repository, the steps are as follows:

1. Right-click on the same file and select **TortoiseGit** and click on **Pull...**:

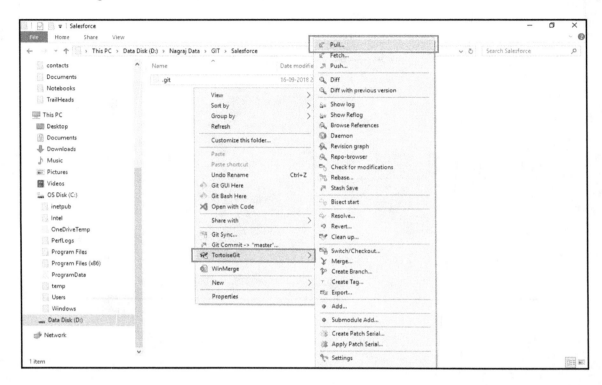

2. You will get one popup, as shown. Select **...** to select **Remote Branch**:

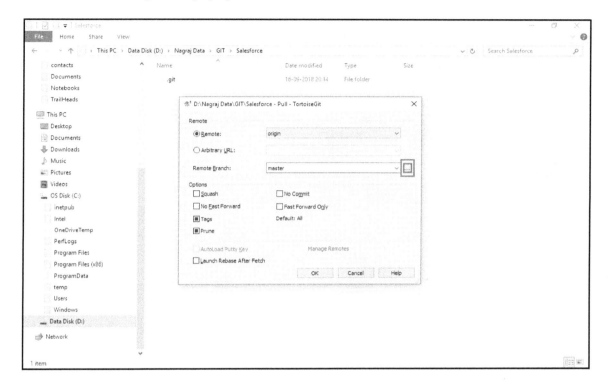

3. Here you can see all the list of remote branches, select the specific branch and click on **OK**:

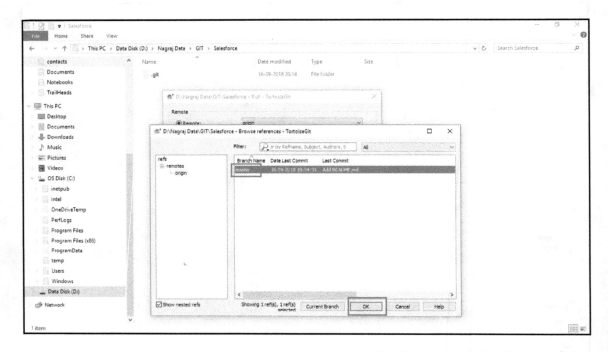

4. Once the process is complete, click on **Close**:

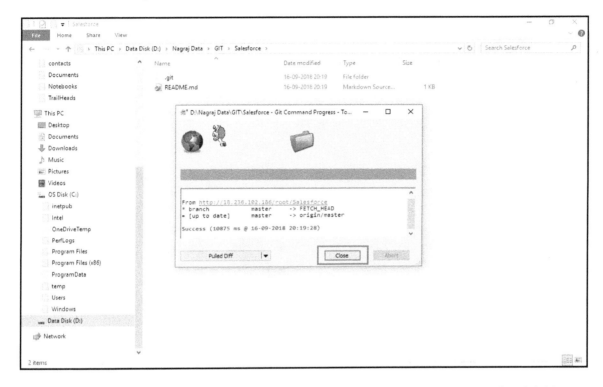

Now the connection has been created and all the files copied to the local folder from the Git repository.

5. Add your files into this folder:

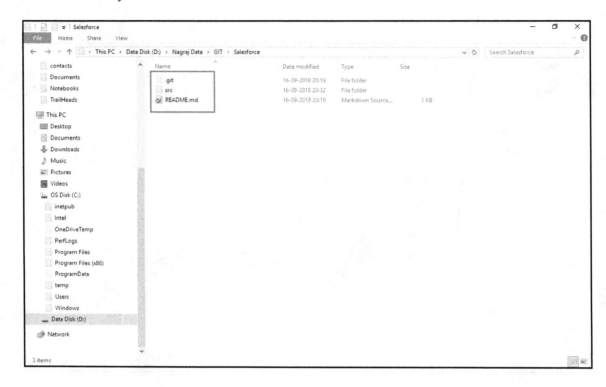

6. Right-click on the same folder and select the **TortoiseGit** and click on **Add...**:

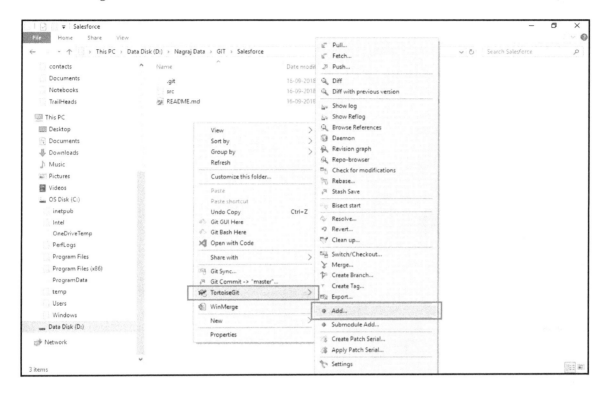

7. Select all the files and click on **OK**:

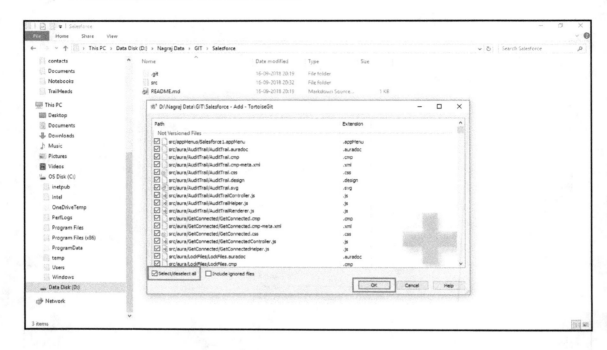

8. Once the process is complete, click on **Commit...**:

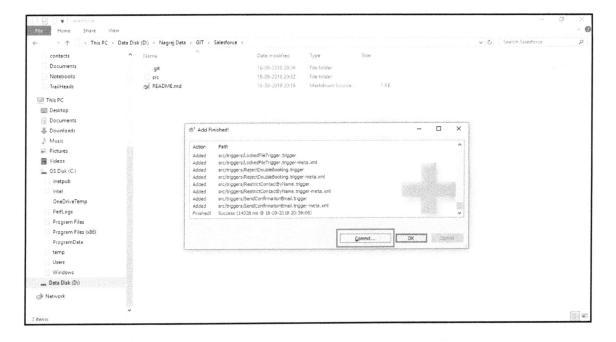

9. Now add the commit message and click on **Commit & Push**:

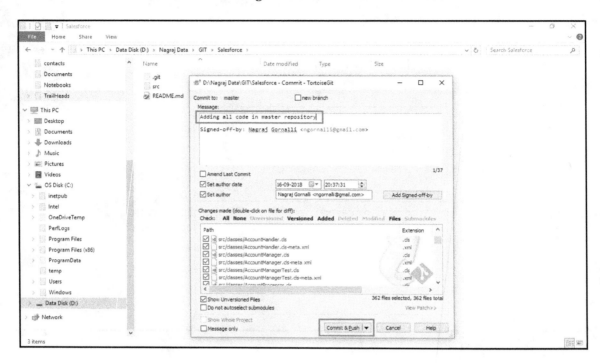

10. To see all the remote branches, select the ... button:

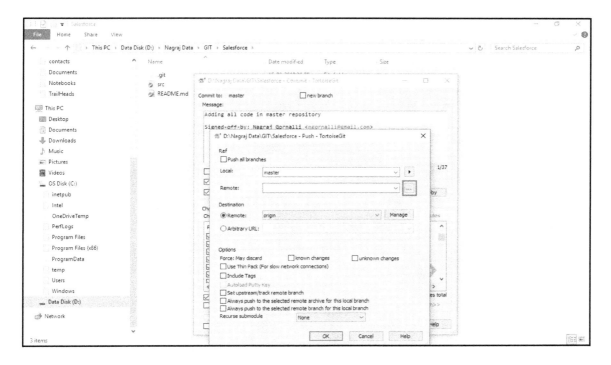

11. Here you see all the branches, select the specific branch:

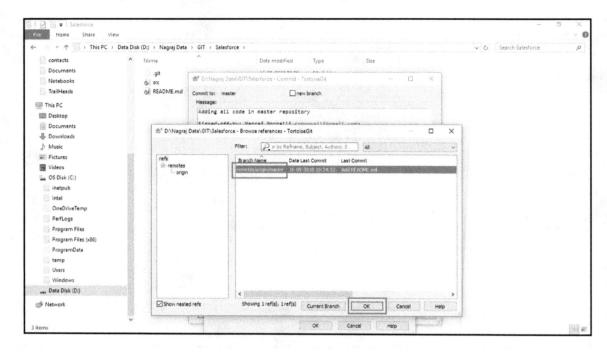

12. Now click on **OK**:

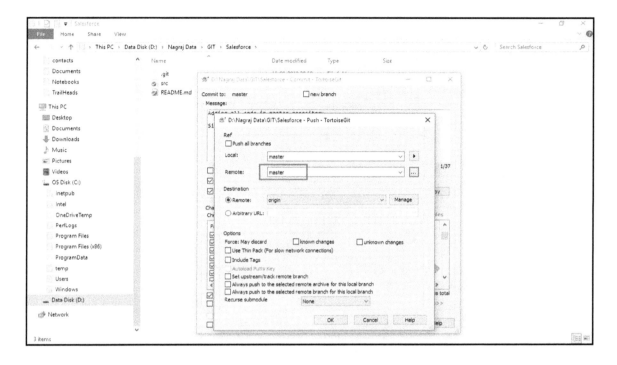

13. Once the process is complete, click on **Close**:

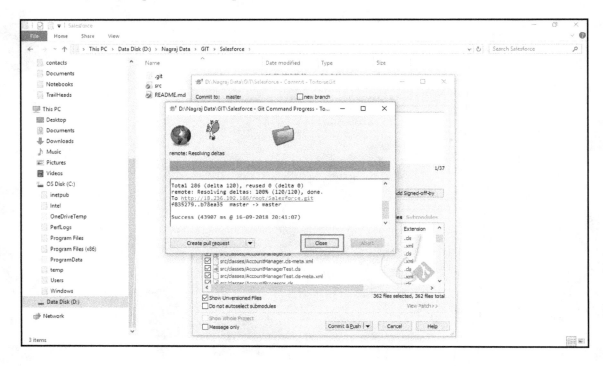

14. Now all the files are moved to the Git repository. Check on the Git repository:

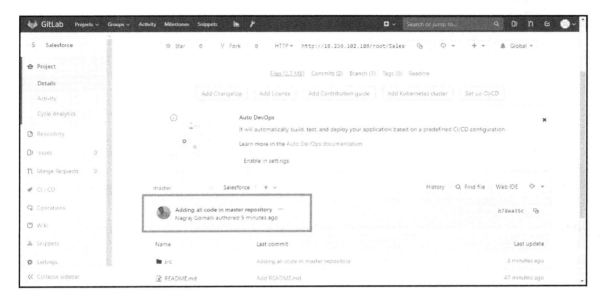

15. Check all the files have been committed correctly:

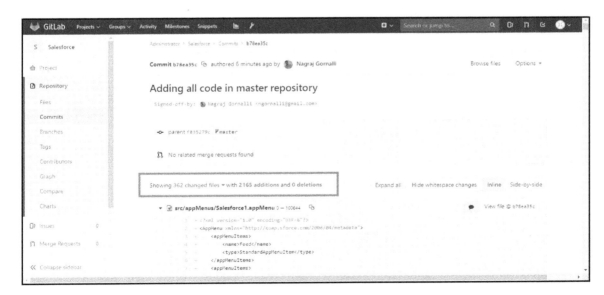

All code is successfully committed in the Git repository.

Summary

In this chapter, we learned about version control systems. We have seen what version control we have in Salesforce and why we need a version control system such as Git. We learned how to install GitLab on on-premise servers using the most recommended method by GitLab itself—the omnibus setup. After setting up our own GitLab server, we learned how to create our first project in GitLab using a web UI. We worked with the Git repository using Git commands, such as `git clone`, `add`, `commit`, `push`, and so on.

We discussed the branching strategy in Git and general scenarios where we need to work with different branches. We have learned about concepts such as protected branch, and default branch. We also got to know how we can create a new branch from an existing branch, and merge code from one branch to another branch. Finally, we learned how to use Git for our Salesforce project with Eclipse.

In the next chapter, we will go to our next stage, which is Continuous Integration using a Jenkins server. We will learn how Jenkins helps us to automate our daily tasks, such as retrieving and deploying metadata using the Force.com migration tool and Git.

Continuous Integration 6

In the previous chapter, we learned about the importance of version control systems in projects and how we can achieve version control in our Salesforce project. We looked at instructions for how to set up our own GitLab server and push metadata from the Salesforce organization to the Git repository. After following the steps to install Git on a developer machine and sync it with the Salesforce sandbox, developers will be able to make and save their changes in the Git repository.

In this chapter, we will learn about how we can use Git integration with Jenkins to automate backups and the deployment of Salesforce metadata. We will discuss Jenkins and look at how continuous integration is achieved in Salesforce using Jenkins and the Ant Migration Tool. We will look at how to configure the Ant Migration Tool with Jenkins and and how to configure a Jenkins job to retrieve metadata from the sandbox. We will cover step-by-step instructions for deploying changes to UAT or a testing environment using Jenkins.

In this chapter, we will cover the following topics:

- What is Jenkins?
- Installing Jenkins
- Configuring the Ant Migration Tool with Jenkins
- Providing sandbox credentials to Jenkins
- Configuring a Jenkins job to retrieve metadata from a sandbox
- Configuring a Jenkins job to deploy metadata on a sandbox

What is Jenkins?

Jenkins is a continuous integration server written in Java. Jenkins is an open source automation server. You can install it on your machine easily. Jenkins can be installed on Windows, macOS, and Linux machines. Jenkins is easily configurable and has many plugins to support continuous integration and deployment. If you have experience of using containers, you can use Docker to install Jenkins using Docker images from the registry.

CI using Jenkins

Continuous integration entails developers pushing their code to a shared repository and testing it using regular builds so that they can detect problems in the code gradually.

 There are several tools that can be used to achieve continuous integration.

Using continuous integration, you can easily back-track where things have gone wrong in the code. If you don't follow continuous integration, it will be more difficult and expensive to detect errors in the code at the production stage.

The following is a list of CI tools:

- Jenkins
- TeamCity
- Travis CI
- Go CD
- Bamboo

In this chapter, we are going to use Jenkins to achieve continuous integration.

Jenkins is an open source, cross-platform CI tool. Jenkins has ability to add plugins, which makes it very flexible and easy to integrate. You can configure CI using the UI as well as commands.

Installing a Jenkins server

Let's start with the Jenkins server installation on a Windows server. Installation on the Linux server has already been covered in `Chapter 2`, *Applying DevOps to Salesforce Applications*. We will cover Jenkins server installation on a Windows machine here so that Windows users can get an idea about the setup.

The following are the hardware and software requirements for installation of the Jenkins server.

The hardware requirements are:

- 256 MB of RAM
- 1 GB of drive space

The software requirements are:

- Java 8
- A web browser: Jenkins is supported by most of popular web browsers, such as Google Chrome, Mozilla Firefox, Microsoft Internet Explorer, and the latest version of Apple Safari

Download the latest Jenkins server package for Windows at the following website `http://mirrors.jenkins.io/windows/latest`. You will get the latest ZIP file on your machine of the version of the Jenkins package.

Once the download is completed, extract the ZIP file and start the installation by double-clicking on the `jenkins.msi` file. Follow the Jenkins setup wizard to complete the Jenkins server installation. Choose the path for the Jenkins server installation and click on **Next**:

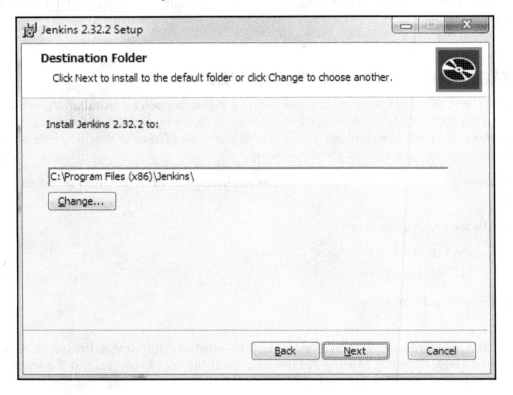

On the next screen, click on **Install** to proceed with the installation:

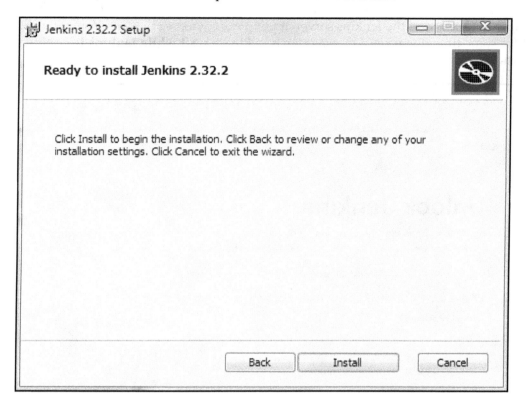

After the Jenkins installation is done, you need to configure the Jenkins server. Visit `http://<Server-IP-address>:8080` if the setup has been done on a local machine for testing. You can access the Jenkins server at `http://localhost:8080`. You will need to wait for some time if you see a message such as **Please wait while Jenkins is getting ready to work...**:

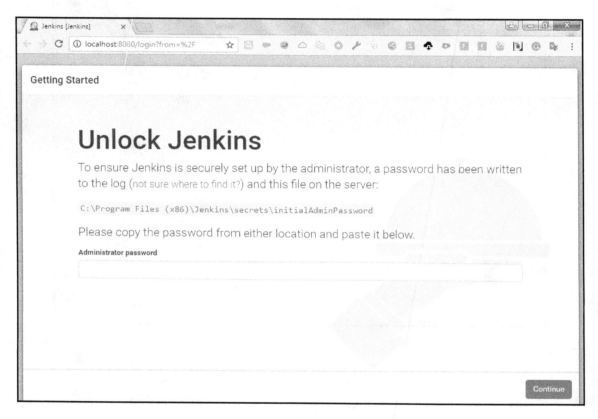

To unlock the Jenkins server, you need to provide the default Jenkins password stored at the following location: `C:\Program Files (x86)\Jenkins\secrets\initialAdminPassword`. For a Linux machine, the path will be different.

On the next screen, we will be able to choose plugins to install in the Jenkins server. Click on **Select plugins to install**:

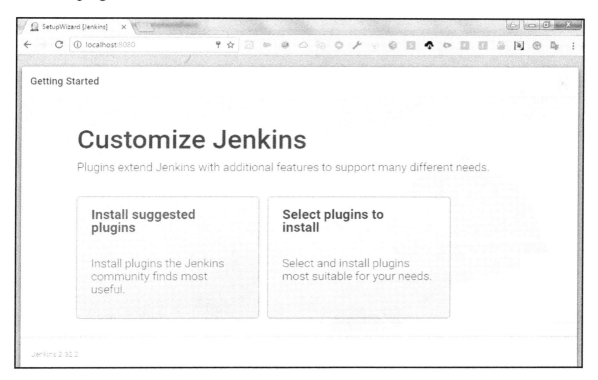

We will only choose **Ant Plugin** and **Git Plugin**, as we can install other plugins after the basic setup is done:

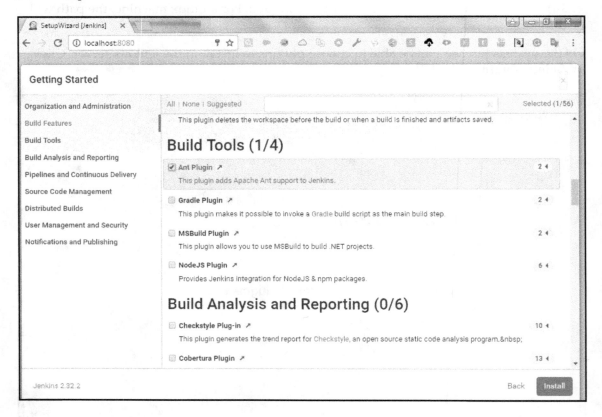

Here is the next page:

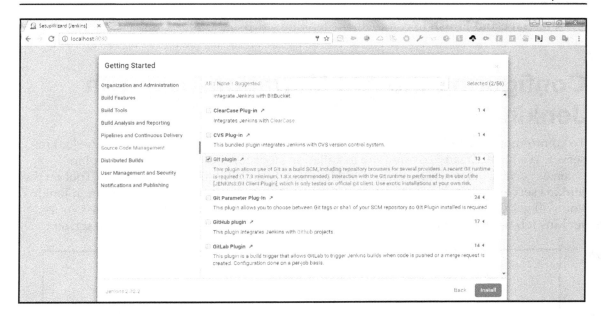

After the plugin installation has been completed, in **Create First Admin User** provide a **Username**, **Password**, **Full name**, and **E-mail address**:

Click on **Save and Finish** to complete the Jenkins setup.

Configuring the Ant Migration Tool with Jenkins

To communicate with Salesforce, we need to install the Ant Migration Tool on the Jenkins server. We have already covered the installation steps for the Ant Migration Tool in `Chapter 4`, *Introduction to the Force.com Migration Tool*. Install the Ant Migration Tool on the Jenkins server and configure the path in Jenkins. Once you install the Ant plugin in Jenkins, you will get the option to **Invoke Ant** in the **Add build step** dropdown menu for your Jenkins Job, which will run `build.xml` and perform the tasks mentioned in the script:

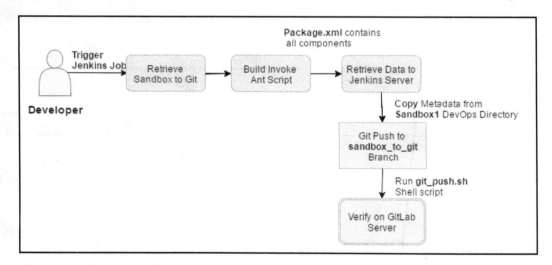

When the developer triggers the Jenkins Job, we will select **Invoke Ant** to retrieve the Salesforce metadata. Once the build is successful, we will have the metadata in the directory and trigger the Jenkins job to push the metadata from Jenkins to the GitLab repository. Verify the metadata in the GitLab repository.

Now we will set the global credentials in Jenkins.

Go to **Manage Jenkins** and select **Global Tool Configuration**. On your machine, the executable file can be different. Go to the **Git** section and provide **Path to Git executable** as shown in the following screenshot:

Configuring a Jenkins job to retrieve metadata from a sandbox

We have created the Git repository with the metadata from the Salesforce Production organization in Chapter 5, *Version Control*. We will use the same sample project and GitLab repository, Salesforce_demo, with the current production code from the Salesforce Sandbox. The instructions are as follows:

1. Create the branch to retrieve code from the sandbox:

   Branch : sandbox_to_git

2. Log in to the Jenkins server and click on **New Item** to create a Jenkins job:

3. Give the name `Retrive_sandbox_to_git` to the Jenkins job. As we are working on an Ant build project, select Build a **Free-style Project**. Click **OK**. The Freestyle project type is used to create a Jenkins project with any SCM using any build system:

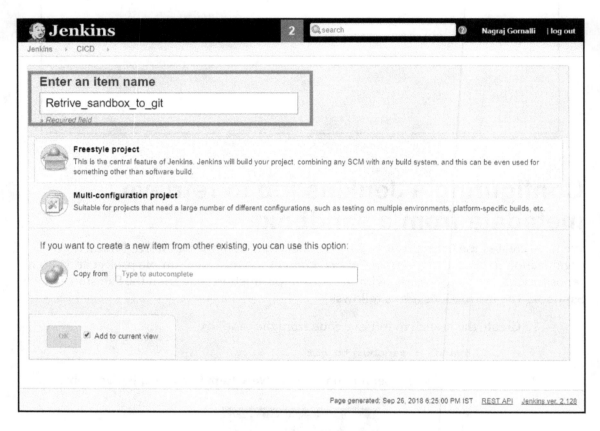

4. Configure the job. After the job has been created, we will go to the job configuration page. In the **General** tab, provide the project name and description, as follows:

- **Project Name**: `Retrive_sandbox_to_git`.
- **Description**: Job to retrieve metadata from sandbox and push to Git.
- **Source Code Management**: Keep it as **None**, as we don't need SCM for this job.
- **Build Triggers**: Do not choose any trigger.
- **Build Environment**: Select Add timestamp to console output if available:

5. Select **Invoke Ant** from the **Add build step** dropdown menu and provide the path for `build.xml` to retrieve the metadata from the sandbox to the Jenkins workspace:

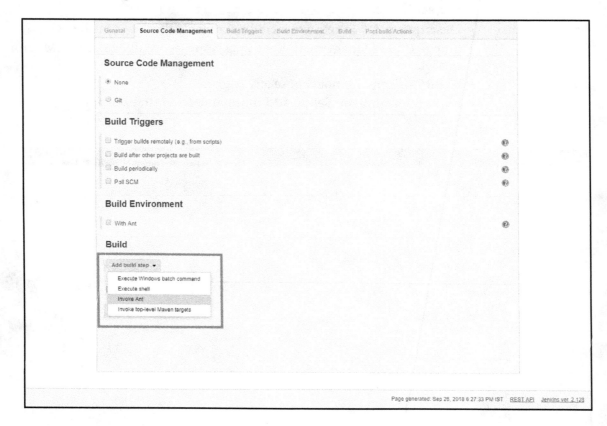

6. Configure the build:
   1. **Targets**: Leave the target empty. Here, you can specify a list of targets you want to run. If we leave it empty, the target specified in the build script will be executed.
   2. **Build File**: The location of `build.xml` is at `<JENKINS_WORKSPACE>/<ITEM-NAME>`. You can specify your build file here; by default Ant will use `build.xml` in the root directory. The workspace root directory is at: `<JENKINS_WORKSPACE>/$ITEM_NAME`. Example: Building in workspace `<JENKoNS_WORKSPACE>/Retrieve_SandBox_to_Git`.
   3. **Java Options**: `<-Xmn1024m>` provide the Java memory limit, because the job will throw error if its less.

The sample `build.xml` is as shown:

```
<project name="Force.com Migration Tool"
default="retrieveUnpackaged" basedir="."
xmlns:sf="antlib:com.Salesforce">
<taskdef uri="antlib:com.Salesforce"
        resource="com/Salesforce/antlib.xml"
        classpath="lib/ant-Salesforce.jar"
    />
    <property file="build.properties"/>
        <property environment="env"/>
        <property name="sf.username"
value="${env.SF_USERNAME}"/>
        <property name="sf.password"
value="${env.SF_PASSWORD}"/>
        <property name="sf.token" value="${env.SF_TOKEN}"/>
        <property name="sf.serverurl"
value="${env.SF_SERVERURL}"/>
            <target name="retrieveUnpackaged">
                <sf:retrieve
                    username="${sf.username}"
                    password="${sf.password}${sf.token}"
                    serverurl="${sf.serverurl}"
                    retrieveTarget="DevOps/src"
                    unpackaged="${basedir}/package.xml"
                />
        </target>
</project>
```

This will retrieve an unpackaged set of metadata from your organization. In `retrieveTarget`, mention the path where the metadata will be stored:

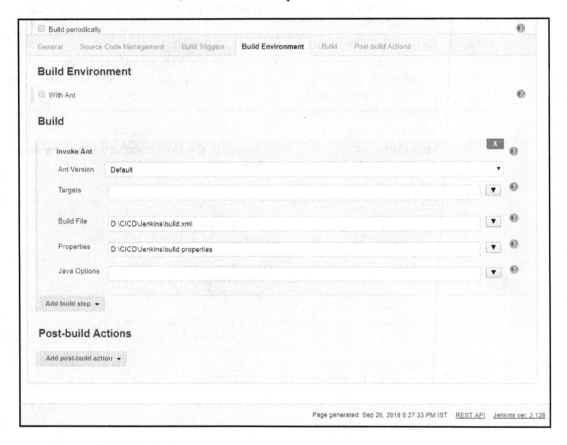

7. In **Post-build Actions**, we will execute a shell script to perform a Git push to the `sandbox_to_git` branch:

- Trigger job `Retrive_SandBox_to_Git2`. It will push all the code retrieved by the `Build.xml` script in `DevOps/src`.
- The following are some sample commands to push code in the Git repository:

```
$git add.
$git commit -m "Retrieve metadata from sandbox"
$git remote add origin <remote-repository-URL>
$git push -u origin sandbox_to_git
```

8. Test the job: Make sure the project is *enabled* in Jenkins. Select it from the list of projects, and click **Build Now**.

   1. Check the **Console Output**. After the build, click **Build Details** and you can also refer to the **Console Output** and check if there are any errors on the build script:

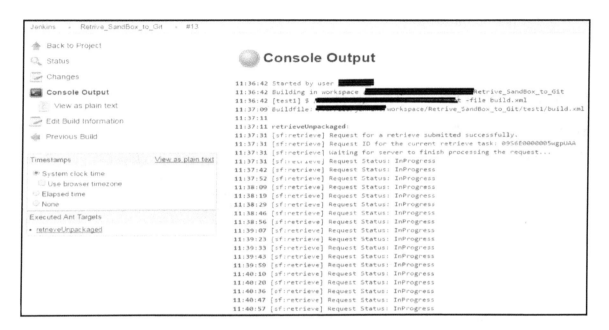

9. Check the Console Output in the Jenkins Console. If the build is successful, then it will show the following message: **BUILD SUCCESSFUL**:

10. Verify the updated code in the Git Branch sandbox_to_git.

Triggering the same job again

To execute the same Jenkins job again, follow these steps:

1. Log in to Jenkins.
2. Select the job that you want to run.
3. Click on **Build Now**.
4. Check the status/console output.

Configuring a Jenkins job to deploy metadata on a sandbox

We have Eclipse with the Force.com IDE and Git installed in it. The developer sandbox is in sync with Eclipse. Developers work with Eclipse and the Force.com IDE. Sandbox will be in sync with the Eclipse workspace. After changes are done, the developer will push changes to the Git branch and mention the deployment component in `package.xml`. This Git push will trigger a Jenkins job that will execute the Ant deploy script and deploy changes from the developer sandbox to test the sandbox:

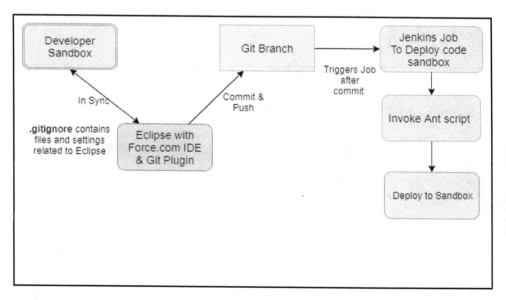

The tools used are:

- **Git**: To track Salesforce changes in Git
- **Force.com Migration Tool**: For Salesforce deployments
- **Jenkins**: To automate deployments to a pre-UAT environment with Jenkins and Ant scripts

The configuration steps are as follows:

1. Create a Jenkins job to deploy code to the sandbox. Log in to the Jenkins server and click on **New Item** to create a Jenkins job:

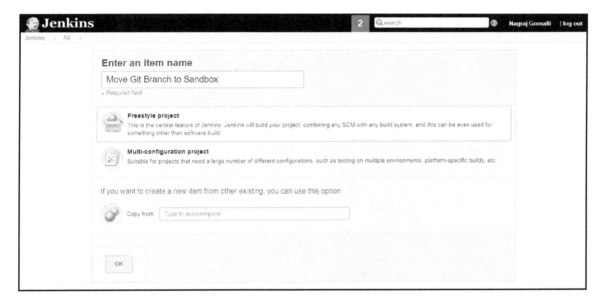

2. Configure **Source Code Management**. Copy the project URL from your Git project and paste it the to **Repository URL**.

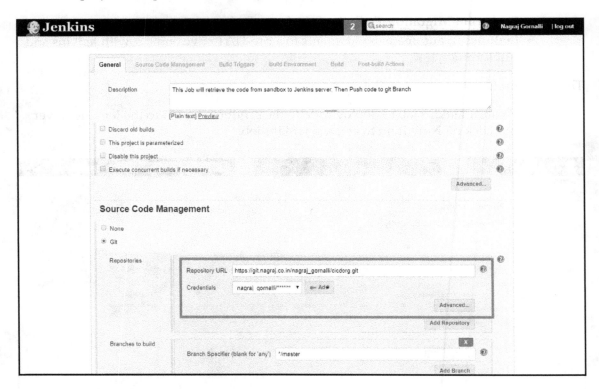

3. Add the credentials for Git access in Jenkins Credentials. Add your username and password and select the following credential:

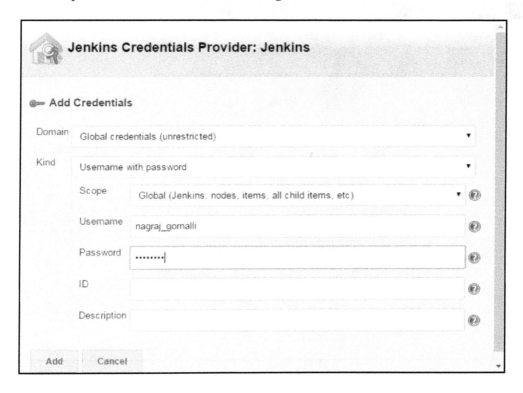

4. Configure the Git credentials and branches you want to build:

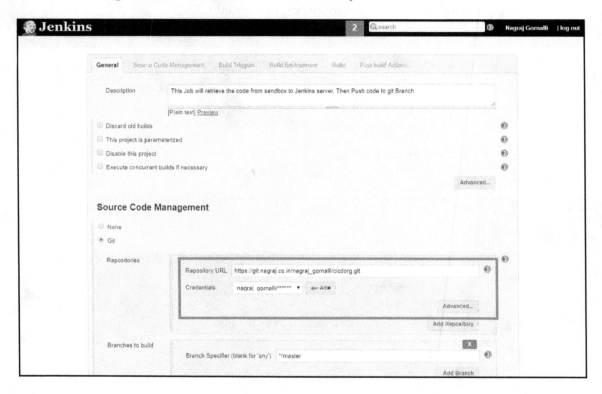

5. Select the build and select **Invoke Ant.** Configure the build file and the `build.properties` file:

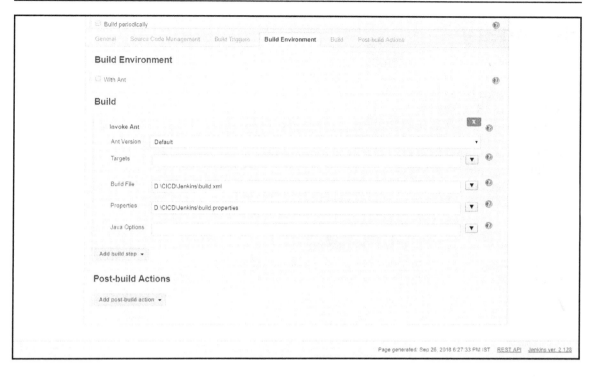

6. The components developers want to deploy will be mentioned in `package.xml` and deployed in the ant job. The sample `Build.xml` for the deploy job is as follows:

```
<target name="deployCode">
    <!-- Deploy Code From src to SandBox -->
        <sf:deploy
            username="${sf.username}"
            password="${sf.password}${sf.token}"
            serverurl="${sf.serverurl}"
            deployroot="src"
                        runAllTests="false"
        />
</target>
```

7. Once developers push the code to the respective Git branch, the Jenkins job will be triggered and the new code is deployed to the destination sandbox. This sandbox can be a UAT sandbox or production. You can use the same job for different scenarios.

Summary

In this chapter, we have learned how to automate backups for Salesforce metadata and push code to the Git repository using Jenkins. Tracking changes in Salesforce is possible with GitLab and Jenkins jobs. We have explained how to configure the Ant Migration Tool with Jenkins and what the flow is for this retrieved code from the sandbox to the Jenkins server so as to push it to the Git branch using the script for backup.

We have learned how to set up our own Jenkins server and configure it to retrieve metadata from our Salesforce sandbox. Also we have configured a Jenkins job for deploying metadata from one sandbox to another sandbox. Regarding the deployment job, we discussed the tools that can be used and explained the flow for deployment to UAT or testing with a diagram.

In the next chapter, we will learn about continuous testing and code coverage in Salesforce. We will discuss the steps to perform tests on Salesforce using Selenium and Qualitia. We will learn about automating the process of continuous testing using Jenkins.

7
Continuous Testing

In the previous chapter, we learned about setting our own Jenkins server and using Jenkins for continuous integration, how to configure Jenkins for retrieving metadata from Salesforce sandbox, and pushing code to Git's version control. We also performed steps to deploy metadata to UAT sandbox, using Jenkins and the Ant migration tool.

In this chapter, we will learn about code quality using PMD. We will discuss continuous testing and executing Apex tests in a deployment using Jenkins. We will get to know Selenium, and how to set up Selenium using Firefox. We will also go through record and playback for the Salesforce sample application. We will discuss using the Qualitia scriptless automation tool with Jenkins, where we get test reports in HTML format.

What is code quality?

Code quality is identify based on some parameters such as best practices standards and rule sets. When code quality is increased, then user acceptance testing issues and production issues are reduced and productivity is increased. Using this PMD report, produced by an open source static source code analyzer that reports on issues found in the code, we can allocate extra time for reviewing code, and this increases product quality, along with best practice standards and effective governance.

Checking code quality using a PMD report

There are two methods for performing the analysis. We will discuss them in the next sections.

PMD static analysis for Salesforce Apex using a Visual Studio (VS) Code extension

Here, we will learn to analyze directly in VS Code on Apex and Visual force files. First, you have to install Visual Studio Code on your machine. (We already learned how to install VS Code in `Chapter 3`, *Deployment in Salesforce*).

You need to perform the following steps:

1. Open Visual Studio Code and click on **Extensions** (*Ctrl + Shift + X*):

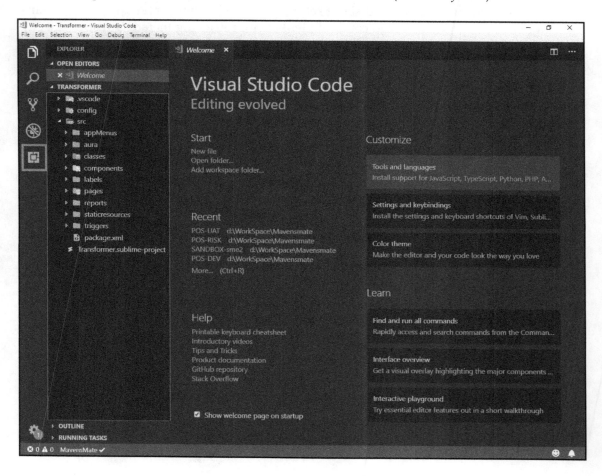

2. In **Search extension in Market Place,** enter pmd:

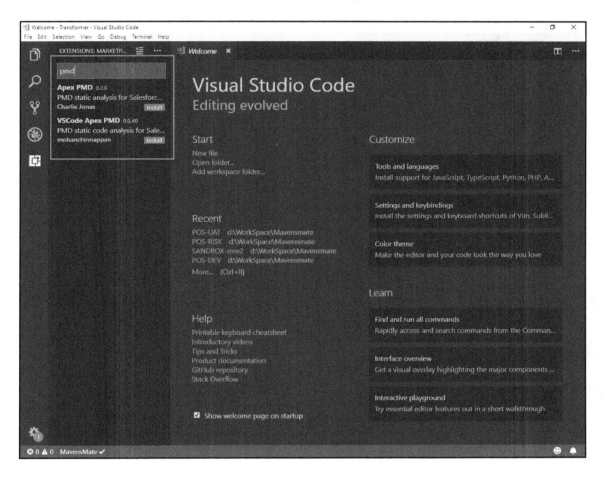

3. Select **Apex PMD** and click **Install**:

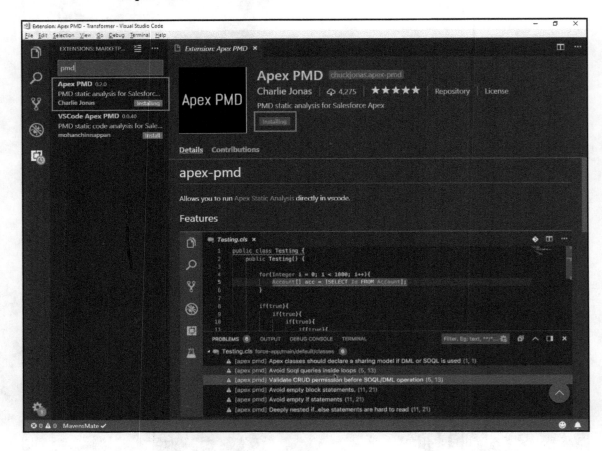

4. Once installation is complete, click **Reload** and this will restart your VS Code:

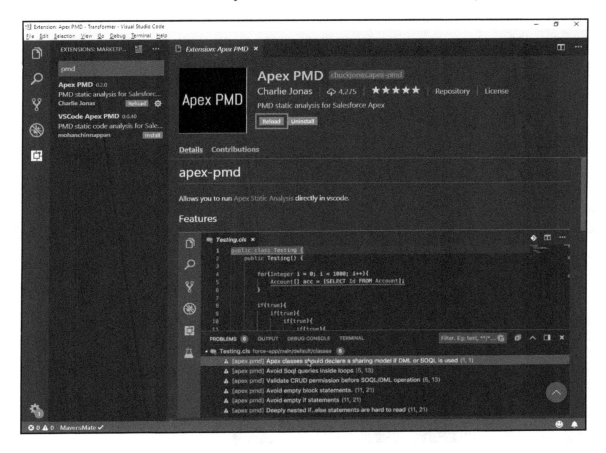

5. Open the file about which you want to analyze the PMD report:

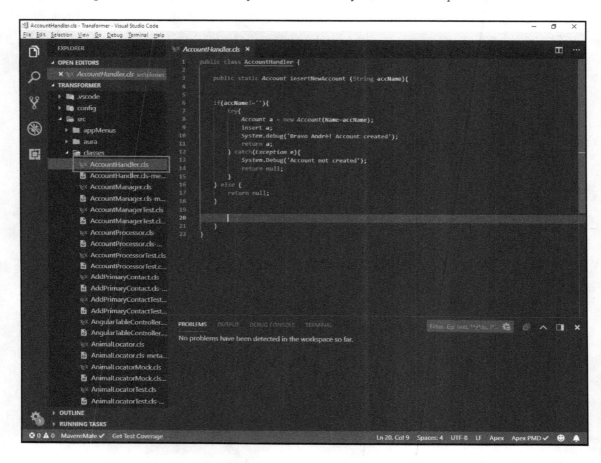

6. Now, open the command panel by right-clicking and selecting **All Commands**, or press *Ctrl + Shift + P*. Enter Apex `stat` in the command panel:

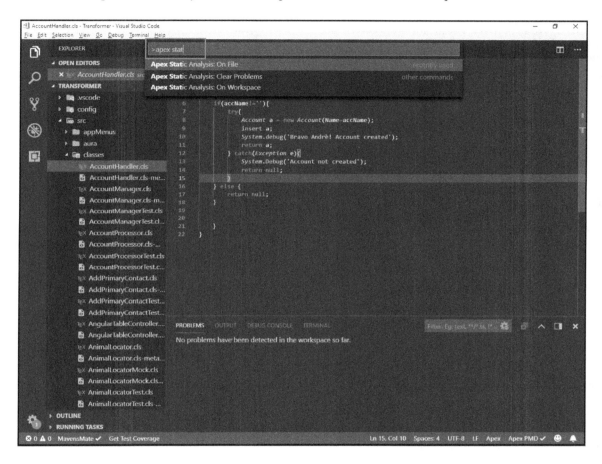

7. Now, click on **Apex Static Analysis: On File**. It shows you all the analytical results in **PROBLEMS**.
8. Resolve all the problems and run **Apex Static Analysis: On File** again.

PMD static analysis for Salesforce Apex using the command line

Here, we can run a PMD analysis on all files by using a single command. The steps are as follows:

1. First, download the PMD JAR file from `https://sourceforge.net/projects/pmd/files/pmd-eclipse/update-site/`, and then take a look at this screenshot:

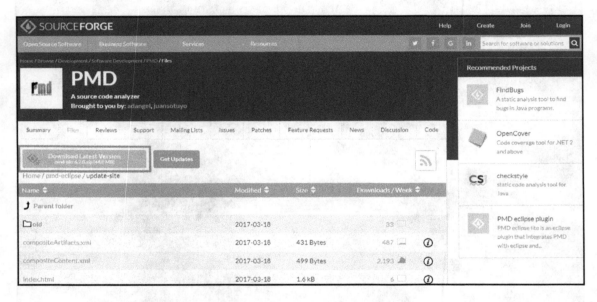

2. Extract the JAR file, go inside the bin file, and copy the path of that folder.
3. Now, open **Run** by pressing Windows + *R* and enter the command to open the command-line panel.
4. Go to your bin path by entering the path of that folder. If you are on another drive, then first go to that drive and enter the copied path:

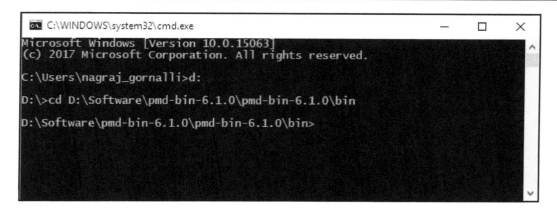

5. Now, create your command:

```
pmd -d "Source Path" -R apex-ruleset -language Apex -f CSV >
"Destination Ptah\ReportName.csv"
//Source Path: Your Project Directory Path till src.
//Destination Path: Report Folder Path where you want to store
the report.
```

6. Then, execute this command:

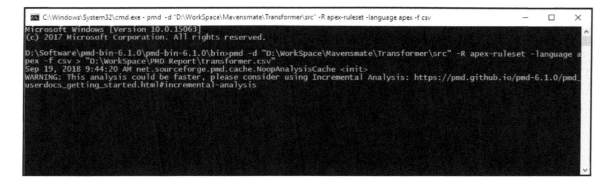

You will get an exported CSV file:

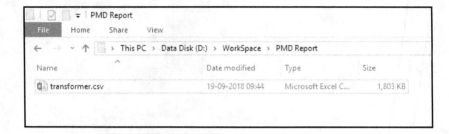

7. Now, open that CSV file and correct your code based on the error types.

In the CSV file, we get following columns:

- **Problem**: This is just a serial number of the problems
- **Package**: In this column, we get the package name of that file
- **File**: In this column, we get the exact file path of that file
- **Priority**: There are different types of priorities, from 1 to 3, and they are added to this column
- **Line**: In this column, we get the exact line number of the problem
- **Description**: In this column, we get a single-line description of the problem
- **Rule set**: In this column, we get the rule set's name
- **Rule**: In this column, we get the rule's name

There are different types of rules and rule sets. Here are some examples of rules and rule sets:

- Best practices:
  - ApexUnitTestClassShouldHaveAsserts
  - AvoidGlobalModifier
  - AvoidLogicInTrigger
- Code style:
  - ClassNamingConventions
  - ForLoopsMustUseBraces
  - IfElseStmtsMustUseBraces
  - IfStmtsMustUseBraces
  - MethodNamingConventions
  - VariableNamingConventions

- Design:
    - AvoidDeeplyNestedIfStmts
    - CyclomaticComplexity
    - ExcessiveClassLength
    - ExcessiveParameterList
    - ExcessivePublicCount
    - NcssMethodCount
    - StdCyclomaticComplexity
    - TooManyFields
- Errors prone:
    - AvoidHardcodingId
    - EmptyCatchBlock
    - EmptyStatementBlock
- Performance:
    - AvoidSoqlInLoops
- Security:
    - ApexCRUDViolation
    - ApexSharingViolations
    - ApexSOQLInjection
    - ApexXSSFromURLParam

Executing Apex tests in a deployment using Jenkins

In Salesforce code, coverage of Apex components should be more than 75% to deploy changes to production. If any test case fails during deployment, then deployment to production will also fail. To avoid this, it is recommended that you test your deployment in sandbox first before deploying it to production. Sometimes, individual code coverage of Apex components may be less than 75%, but overall code coverage for your organization should be 75% or more. To ensure test cases don't fail in production, you can execute a subset of test cases in sandbox after it's deployed. We have already seen deploying changes from one sandbox to another in the previous chapter. We just need to make small changes in build.xml to specify the subset of tests to execute while deploying.

Here is a sample `build.xml` with test cases to execute:

```
<target name="deployCode">
    <sf:deploy username="${sf.username}" password="${sf.password}"
            sessionId="${sf.sessionId}" serverurl="${sf.serverurl}"
            deployroot="codepkg" testLevel="RunSpecifiedTests">
        <runTest>TestClassSample1</runTest>
        <runTest>TestClassSample2</runTest>
        <runTest>TestClassSample3</runTest>
    </sf:deploy>
</target>
```

To run specific tests, the value of the `testLevel` parameter should be set to `RunSpecifiedTests`. A child element, `</runTest>`, is used to specify the test classes to run.

To run all test cases from `sf:deploy` tasks with the `runAllTests="true"` attribute, `package.xml` should be empty, as shown here:

```
<?xml version="1.0" encoding="UTF-8"?> <Package
xmlns="http://soap.sforce.com/2006/04/metadata"> <version>42.0</version>
</Package>
```

Here is a sample `build.xml` used to run all test cases:

```
<target name="deployCode">
    <!-- Deploy Code From src to sandBox -->
    <sf:deploy
        username="${sf.username}"
        password="${sf.password}${sf.token}"
        serverurl="${sf.serverurl}"
        deployroot="src"
        runAllTests="true"
    />
</target>
```

The role of Jenkins in deployment will be the same; developers just need to change the parameters in the `build.xml` and the `package.xml` configuration files.

What is continuous testing?

Continuous testing is the process of executing test cases after new changes are deployed to the environment. In continuous testing, we evaluate deployments at every stage so that any bugs introduced in the existing code are reported earlier in the software development cycle. Software changes are continuously moved from the development to the test environment, and the testing team needs to test all the existing functionalities, along with new functionalities. Manual testing takes a longer time to complete, and feedback from the testing team is required to make further decisions about application delivery. Continuous testing helps us to get immediate feedback and makes the testing cycle easier. Having continuous testing in place reduces the business risk involved in releasing software with bugs:

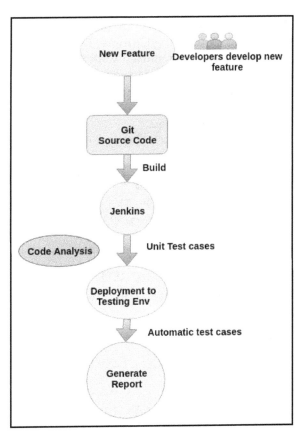

Continuous testing is dein the preceding diagram. Whenever any new feature is developed by the development team, developers push code in a source code versioning system such as Git, so that the changes are tracked. Once a feature is ready in the development environment, it is moved to a continuous integration server such as Jenkins. Jenkins will build the source code, and once the build is deployed to the test environment, we will configure the Jenkins job to execute the test cases. For continuous testing, we can use tools to write and execute automation test cases, such as Selenium, Katalon Studio, Qualitia, and so on. In this chapter, we will only focus on the Selenium testing framework.

Introducing Selenium

Selenium is an open source tool used for automating tests we run on a web application. Selenium is a web-based application. We can automate the testing using Selenium. Selenium supports many browsers, including Chrome, Firefox, and Safari. You don't need scripting or development knowledge to get started with Selenium, a person with administration experience can also start setting up Selenium. Using a record/playback tool in Selenium, we can perform tests without knowledge of the scripting language. Selenium supports multiple platforms, including Windows, Linux, and Mac. We are going to look at the steps to set up Selenium on Mac.

Setting up Selenium using Firefox

We will set up Selenium with Firefox on macOS. The installation steps for Firefox might differ, depending on your operating system. We will be using Mac in this example.

Here are some prerequisites for installing Firefox on Mac:

- Operating systems: macOS 10.9, 10.10, 10.11, 10.12, and 10.13
- Recommended hardware: Macintosh computer with an Intel x86 processor
- 512 MB of RAM
- 200 MB hard drive space

The installation steps are as follows:

1. Visit `https://www.mozilla.org/firefox/new/?utm_medium=referralandutm_source=support.mozilla.org`. It will automatically detect the platform you are using and provide a download link in the browser.
2. Click the download button; it will start downloading Firefox.
3. Once the download is complete, open the `Firefox.dmg` file.
4. Drag and drop Firefox into the applications folder:

It will start copying the `Firefox.dmg` file to **Applications**:

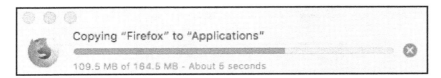

5. Open Firefox from **Applications**. You will see a warning that Firefox is being installed from the internet. Click on **Open**.

6. We have Firefox installed on our system. We can skip email verification in Firefox. Open `https://www.seleniumhq.org/download/` in Firefox.

7. Go to the **Selenium IDE** section and click on the **For Firefox** link. It will redirect you to the **Add Selenium IDE** extension page:

Selenium IDE

Selenium IDE is a Chrome and Firefox plugin which records and plays back user interactions with the browser. Use this to either create simple scripts or assist in exploratory testing.

Download latest released version for Chrome or for Firefox or view the Release Notes.

Download previous IDE versions here.

---

8. Click on **Add to Firefox**:

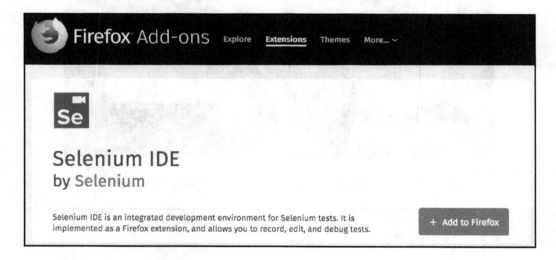

9. This extension require some permissions to work. Click on **Add**:

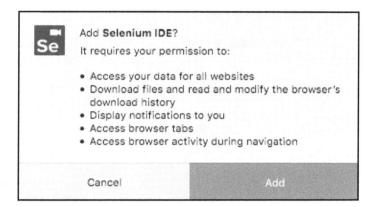

10. Once the **Selenium IDE** plugin is added, you will see the popup:

11. Once the **Selenium IDE** plugin is installed in Firefox, you can launch it by clicking on the **Selenium IDE** icon in the top-right corner:

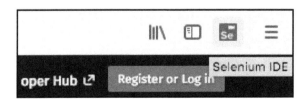

Recording tests using Selenium

The steps to record tests are as follows:

1. Once Selenium is launched, you will see the following window. Provide the base URL as `https://login.salesforce.com` and click on **Start Recording**:

2. Every action you perform in Firefox will be tracked by Selenium. Open `https://login.salesforce.com`, provide a username and password to log in, and click on **Login**:

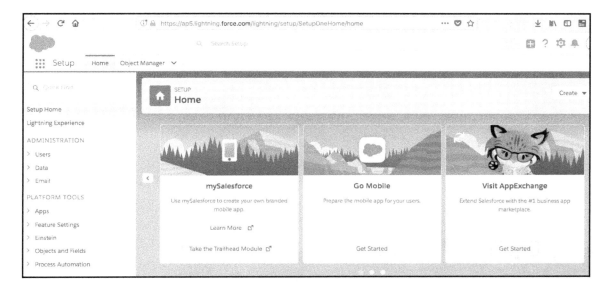

3. Once logged in, you can click on any item or perform any action. You will see a notification about commands being recorded by Selenium:

4. After performing the task, click on **Logout**. You can see the steps being recorded by Selenium in this screenshot:

You can see the commands stored in the Selenium IDE:

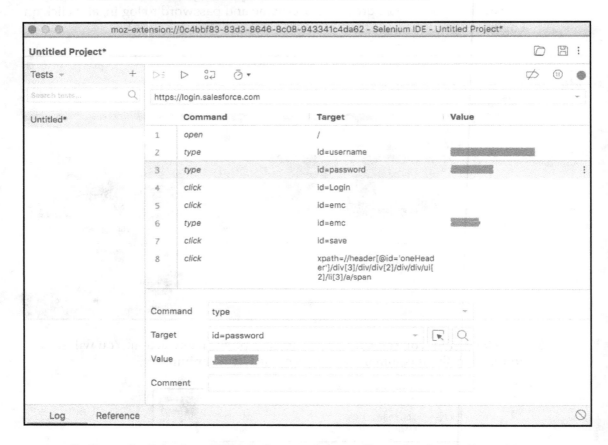

5. Go to the Selenium IDE window, and you will see the data collected by Selenium. Click on **Stop Recording**:

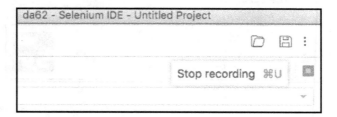

6. Save the recording under any name, for example, `Sample`. You can keep the names specific to the tests you performed as a meaningful naming convention:

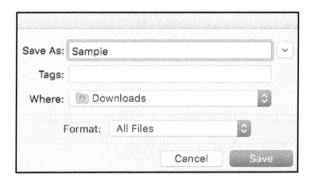

Playing back the recorded tests using Selenium

A record step is completed by Selenium. Now, we can use the same file to re-run the steps. This process is called **playback**:

1. Open **Selenium IDE** from the Firefox browser.
2. Click on **Open Project**:

3. Browse to the file we stored in the record step as `Sample.side`. Open this file and click on **Run Current Test**:

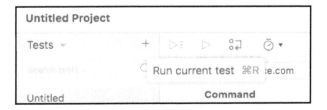

4. Selenium will open Salesforce UEL and perform steps from the sample test case. Log in to Salesforce and log out after performing the test case.

5. Check the logs in Selenium's **Log** console:

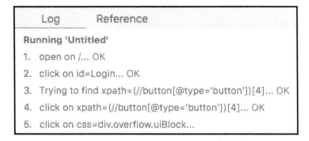

6. Click on **Stop Test execution** if you want to stop execution:

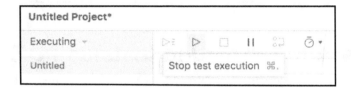

We can write test cases in any language and execute test cases after deploying to Salesforce sandbox. Selenium can be used to automate tests. Whenever we deploy code from the development sandbox to the UAT sandbox or from sandbox, to production, we can execute test cases with Selenium to cover each and every scenario and make sure the application is bug-free. Manually testing all functionality can take a long time, and we end up having longer testing cycles. Releasing changes to production frequently involves a lot of testing and feedback loops to ensure the quality of the application.

We can create a Jenkins job for the execution of test cases with Selenium on the deployment sandbox. If the sandbox is not a full-copy sandbox, then we might need to add some test data, change email IDs of users, and so on. For such tasks, we can use Selenium to automate and speed up the process of software testing and delivery.

Introducing Qualitia

Qualitia is a scriptless testing tool. Qualitia is a functional test automation platform that provides us with a way to automate testing without scripting. Qualitia integrates with Jenkins as well. Qualitia is based on Selenium, in that it doesn't require you to write any scripts. After executing test cases in sandbox, Qualitia presents the results for the test cases in HTML format so that they are readable by the end user. We can host these HTML files on a file server and developers and testers will be able to access them using web browser.

Qualitia provides integration with Jenkins. We can execute automated test cases after deploying to the UAT sandbox. Also, we will be able to schedule our automated tests once per day in our pre-production or staging sandbox.

Running test cases with Qualitia

To run test cases with Qualitia, we need to integrate it with Jenkins. Qualitia's job will be executed on the Windows server, so if we don't have Jenkins on the Windows server, then we can add the Windows client to the Jenkins server and run Qualitia test cases on it. We need the Qualitia JAR and path to the XML test cases and Chrome's driver in order to execute tests. Qualitia will run a test case sandbox and generate reports in HTML.

Use case – continuous testing using Qualitia

The following diagram shows the integration of open source tools with Salesforce sandbox and provides versioning, scriptless testing, and automated deployments using GitLab, the Force.com Migration tool, Jenkins, and Qualitia:

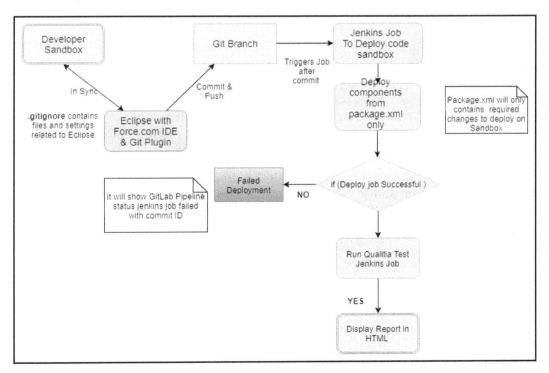

In the previous scenario, developers work with Eclipse and the Force.com IDE. sandbox will be in sync with the Eclipse workspace. After the changes are complete, the developer will push changes to Git and mention the components to be deployed in the `package.xml` file. This Git push will trigger the Jenkins job, which will execute the Ant deployment script and deploy changes from the developer's sandbox to the test sandbox. If our deployment is successful, then it will trigger another job to run Qualitia tests, creating a report in HTML format.

Here is a list of the tools used:

- **Git**: For tracking Salesforce changes in Git
- **Force.com Migration tool**: For Salesforce deployments
- **Jenkins**: To automate deployments to the pre-UAT environment, with Jenkins and an Ant script
- **Qualitia**: Scriptless testing tool

 Note: We can use Selenium for automation testing instead of Qualitia.

Summary

In this chapter, we learned about code quality and continuous testing. We discussed the tools used in automation testing, such as Selenium and Qualitia. We learned the step-by-step process for setting up Selenium with Firefox. We performed a test case on a sample Salesforce application, using record and playback in Selenium.

We discussed use cases for the Qualitia scriptless automation tool, used to perform tests on the Salesforce application and store the results of automation tests in HTML format. We demonstrated a use case of using a diagram with Git for version control Jenkins as a continuous integration server, and Qualitia for executing automation tests on a Salesforce application. We can replace Qualitia with Selenium if we wish to.

8
Tracking Application Changes and the ROI of Applying DevOps to Salesforce

In this chapter, we will discuss how we can track application changes using open source technologies, such as the Git source control versioning system. We will learn the basics of Bugzilla and how to track issues when they are reported by a tester or user until the fix for the issue/feature is deployed to production.

We will also see how to add some post-build steps in Jenkins to report the build status to Git. This will allow developers to get information about the build status related to every commit. We will discuss how DevOps helps any Salesforce organization to deliver applications faster and what the ROI is from applying DevOps to Salesforce.

How to track application changes

Tracking application changes without a version control system is like finding a needle in a haystack. We have seen how to use GitLab to track application changes in Chapter 5, *Version Control*. Whenever bugs are reported by testers, we use a bug tracker such as Bugzilla to track the life cycle of a bug—from identifying it until the fix is released to production. When a new bug or feature is added to the bug tracker, it is assigned to a developer and the developer starts working on that fix or new feature. Code changes are tracked in Git repositories when developers commit changes to the respective feature branch. The **develop** branch commit message should contain the bug ID to identify the changes done with respect to a particular bug or feature.

If a new feature is added or an issue is fixed, developers can add meaningful commit messages to help us track changes for a new functionality. When we want to merge changes to develop a branch or perform cherry-picks on commits, this becomes easy with meaningful commit messages with a bug ID.

Introducing Bugzilla

Bugzilla bug tracking is an open source bug tracking system. Using Bugzilla, you can create a bug and track that bug until it is closed. Bugzilla provides project management and issue tracking features. Bugzilla is used to improve performance and scalability. Other features include an advanced query application that can remember your searches and integrated email capabilities.

First, you have to install Bugzilla on your system or server, from where you can access Bugzilla using a web browser. The steps are as follows:

1. You can install Bugzilla on a machine from `https://www.bugzilla.org/docs/4.4/en/html/installation.html`.

2. Now open Bugzilla through your browser; the screen looks like the following:

3. Click on **Log In** and enter the credentials. Once you have logged in, the page will look like this:

4. Now click on **User Preferences** or on **Administration** to open the admin panel.
5. Once the admin panel is opened, click on **Users**:

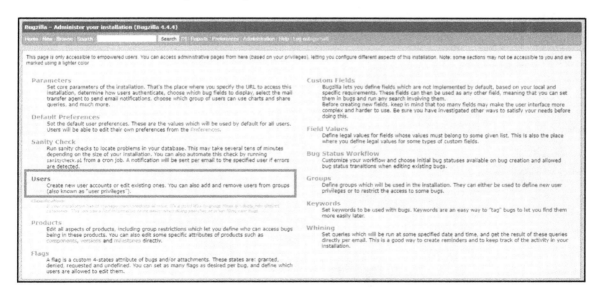

6. In the next screen, click on **add a new user**:

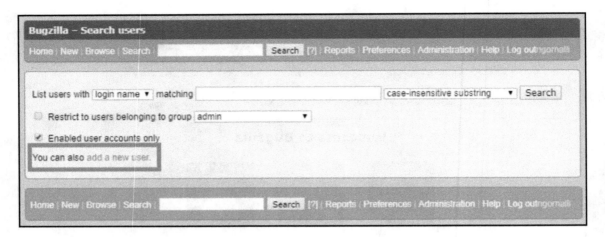

7. Enter the **Login name**, **Password**, and **Real name**. Finally, click on **Add**:

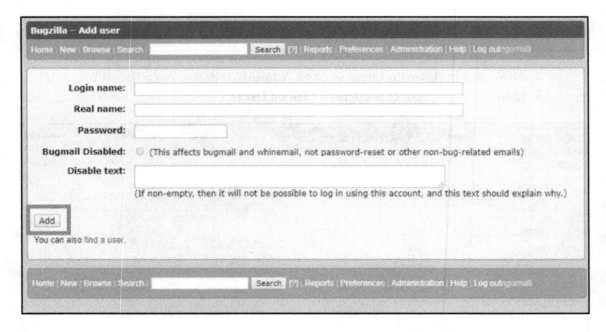

8. Select the relevant accesses and click on **Save Changes**:

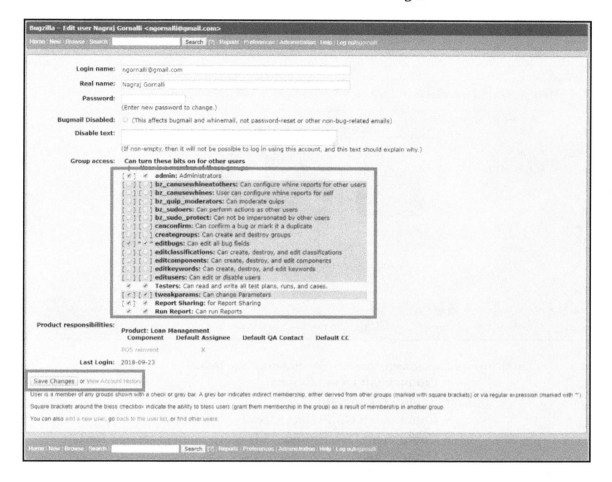

9. Now click on **File a Bug** on the home page:

In the following screen, you can see the multiple fields:
- **Product: Git Demo Project**
- **Reporter: ngornalli**
- **Component: Git Project Model**
- **Component Description: This component is created for Git Demo Project**
- **Version: 1.0**
- **Severity: High**
- **Hardware: Other**
- **OS: Windows**
- **Org*: Transformer**
- **Type of the Ticket*: Defect**
- **Raised By: QA**
- **Steps to Reproduce Issue*: Steps to reproduce issue**
- **Expected Result*: Expected Result**

- **Summary: New Defect added for Git Demo Project**
- **Description: Description**
- **Attachment:** If there is any screenshot then attach it here

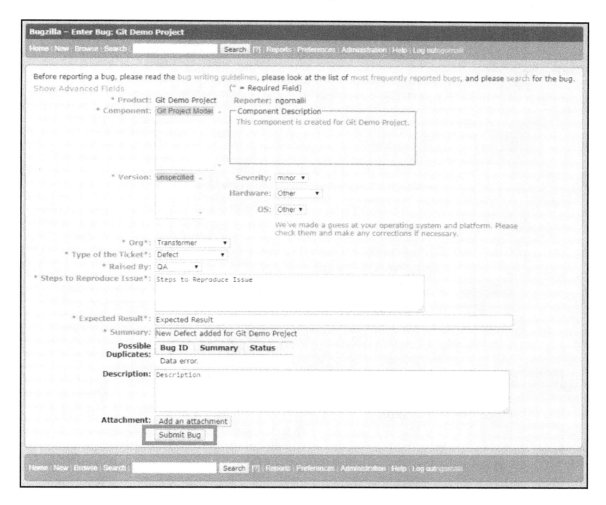

10. Finally, click on **Submit Bug**.

Publishing a build report to Git

As we have seen in `Chapter 6`, *Continuous Integration,* we can trigger a Jenkins job as code is pushed to Jenkins using a Git Webhook. Jenkins will start the build using the Ant Migration Tool and deploy metadata to the sandbox. However, whether the build failed or is successful is not shown anywhere. So we need to change the Jenkins job to deploy changes from Git to the sandbox. Go to the Jenkins job that you want to change and click on **Configure**.

Add the post-build **Git Publisher** step to set the build status to Git commit:

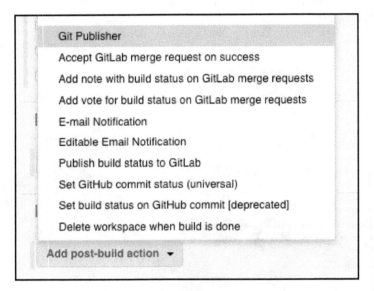

In GitLab, you can view the status of the Jenkins job to check whether is successful or it failed. We can track each commit in Git and see if the deployment to the sandbox step build has passed. If we configure the Jenkins job to run automation test cases after deployment is done in testing the sandbox, we can get the status of the execution of automation test cases in Git:

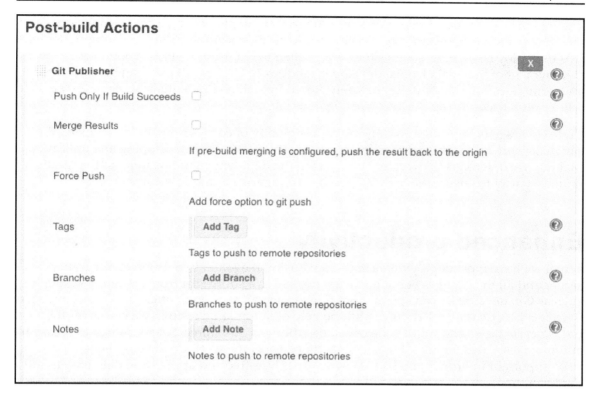

How DevOps helps organizations deliver quickly

Version control helps us track issues and revert changes. Differentiating between branches becomes easy with GitLab. If something goes wrong, finding a bug or issue is easy as we have all the changes tracked in Git repositories. Also, with Jenkins being able to retrieve metadata from the sandbox and store it in Git, it is very useful while taking backups. We don't need to do the same task again. We can configure a Jenkins job to take a backup of metadata components in Git and send a notification email to the respective admins.

The Jenkins continuous integration server helps us to deploy changes from a developer's machine to the sandbox or from one sandbox to another sandbox. We can configure Jenkins jobs to deploy changes as soon as they are pushed to Git using Jenkins Webhooks. Deployment of metadata from a developer sandbox to UAT sandboxes can be automated and your Salesforce credentials are safely stored in Jenkins Credentials in secret text, which will be only used during execution of a Jenkins job.

Code coverage is important for improving the quality of code written by developers. We can make sure that standard practices are being followed while developing an application. Making use of Jenkins to execute Apex tests in the deployment of metadata to the sandbox is an easy way to ensure we have 75% code coverage as per the Salesforce criteria.

Enhanced productivity

When we have most deployments automated using the Jenkins continuous integration server and all the changes being made are tracked in a source control versioning system such as Git, developers can spend more time on actual development tasks. As we have seen in Chapter 7, *Continuous Testing*, with the help of automation testing, we can cover the testing cycle faster and fulfill code coverage criteria in Salesforce. Selenium makes it easy to automate test cases. Finding bugs in an early phase of the software development cycle is very important in order to make sure software is bug-free and application deliverables are deployed to production faster.

How to measure ROI?

Applying DevOps methodologies to Salesforce using open source tools, such as GitLab, Jenkins, Selenium, and so on, helps organizations set up their automation process at minimal cost and with minimal efforts (in doing a one-time setup and configuration).

ROI cannot be measured as a number, but the ROI from applying DevOps can be measured as of the time we save in the deployment of Salesforce and the rework we do whenever developers accidentally overwrite each others' changes. Identifying issues faster with automation testing in the early stages of software development makes it easy to fix issues. Fixing defects in production costs us more time than fixing bugs early in a test or pre-production environment. Having a bug in production will have a business impact on our application.

The reduced time in the maintenance window when we are deploying changes to production and the reduced number of issues in production help us to measure the ROI from applying DevOps to our Salesforce organization. The release cycle can be reduced from weeks to days with automated test cases using Jenkins continuous integration.

By applying DevOps practices to a Salesforce application, we can achieve customer satisfaction and speed up the product delivery process. Developers need to work less hard at maintaining an application, focusing more on developing new features.

Summary

In this chapter, we learned about tracking application changes, Bugzilla, enhancing productivity, and measuring ROI.

We started this book with very basic or no knowledge of DevOps practices or tools used in DevOps. We learned some basics about Salesforce by creating a sample application in Salesforce and discussed the different sandbox environments. Using Eclipse with Salesforce, we can integrate Git with a sandbox to achieve a source control version system. We learned about different deployment methods used in Salesforce, and we automated Salesforce deployments using the Jenkins continuous integration server.

We learned about setting up our own GitLab server and pushing code changes from a Salesforce sandbox to a GitLab repository. Implementing continuous integration in a Salesforce environment with the Jenkins server helps us to speed up deployment to UAT or another sandbox.

We learned how to automate testing for a Salesforce application with Selenium. We discussed Selenium record and playback with a sample Salesforce application. Automation testing helped us reduce the testing cycle from days to hours. We saw how DevOps tools can be used in a Salesforce application. You can apply the concepts learned in this book to any Salesforce application. Throughout this book, we tried to provide you with good insights into DevOps tools and step-by-step instructions to set up your own DevOps process with open source tools. Most of the exercises in this book can be followed using a free Salesforce account.

Other Books You May Enjoy

If you enjoyed this book, you may be interested in these other books by Packt:

Salesforce Lightning Cookbook
Syed Chand Shah

ISBN: 978-1-78953-825-0

- Enable and configure a Lightning solution
- Create standard Lightning solutions and build a basic page layout
- Add custom components to your Lightning pages
- Build and migrate reports and dashboards
- Integrate Lightning pages with Visualforce to enhance performance
- Add stunning custom designs and styling with Lightning Design System

Practical DevOps - Second Edition
Joakim Verona

ISBN: 978-1-78839-257-0

- Understand how all deployment systems fit together to form a larger system
- Set up and familiarize yourself with all the tools you need to be efficient with DevOps
- Design an application suitable for continuous deployment systems with DevOps in mind
- Store and manage your code effectively using Git, Gerrit, Gitlab, and more
- Configure a job to build a sample CRUD application
- Test your code using automated regression testing with Jenkins Selenium
- Deploy your code using tools such as Puppet, Ansible, Palletops, Chef, and Vagrant

Leave a review - let other readers know what you think

Please share your thoughts on this book with others by leaving a review on the site that you bought it from. If you purchased the book from Amazon, please leave us an honest review on this book's Amazon page. This is vital so that other potential readers can see and use your unbiased opinion to make purchasing decisions, we can understand what our customers think about our products, and our authors can see your feedback on the title that they have worked with Packt to create. It will only take a few minutes of your time, but is valuable to other potential customers, our authors, and Packt. Thank you!

Index

www.ingramcontent.com/pod-product-compliance
Lightning Source LLC
Chambersburg PA
CBHW080524060326
40690CB00022B/5023